PONTUS EUXINUS

Amazo[illegible]

MARE HYRCANUM sive CASPIUM

SOGDIA

SABAZA

Memaceni.

Dai.

Aby Scyth barbarorum

MARGIANA.

BACTRIANA.

HYRCANIA.

Tapori.

Arimaspi.

Parthyene.

PARTHIA.

ZARANGAE

EVERGETAE

PAROPAMISUS

Assaceni.

Thyrrei.

ARACHOSIA.

DRANGIANA.

PAR

GEDROSIA.

Sogdy

MEDI PARA

PALAESTINA

AEGYPTUS.

CAE PARS

Bythemanei.

MADIAN, MADIANITAE

RUBRUM MARE.

SABA.

ERYTHRAEUM sive RUBRUM Mare,
sic dictum non à colore, sed ab Erythro rege.
Extatque haud procul à continente insula quaedam,
palmetis frequentibus consita, & in medio ferè
nemore columna, continet regis Erythri
monumentum, literis gentis eius inscriptum,
teste Q. Curtius. Oaracta vocatur haec insula,
apud Arrianum. Hoc mare margaritiferum
esse scribunt Plinius, Aelianus, Philostratus, aliique

ALEXANDRI MAGNI

ALEXANDER THE GREAT

Who Conquered The World by The Age of 32

Rev. Angel Rumano

Astrolog Publishing House

Cover Design: Na'ama Yaffe
Language Consultant: Marion Duman, Carole Koplow
Layout and Graphics: Daniel Akerman
Production Manager: Dan Gold

P.O. Box 1123, Hod Hasharon 45111, Israel
Tel: 972-9-7412044
Fax: 972-9-7442714

ISBN 965-494-175-9

Published by Astrolog Publishing House 2004

Timeline

356 B.C. —— Alexander was born in Pella. His father was Phillip II, the king and general who conquered Greece.

343 B.C. —— Aristotle was hired to tutor Alexander.

340 B.C. —— Alexander's education ended. He was called by his father to fulfill his duties in the government

338 B.C. —— Alexander commanded the cavalry during the Battle of Chaeronea. This battle brought Greece under the control of Macedonia.

336 B.C. —— Philip was murdered by one of his bodyguards. Alexander became the king of Macedonia.

336 B.C. —— Some Greek cities rebelled under the Macedonian rule.

335 B.C. —— Alexander's army stormed the city of Thebes and demolished it, because it had been revolting.

334 B.C. —— Alexander led an attack on Persia.

333 B.C. —— Alexander reached the coast of Syria. The Battle at Issus took place.He defeated the king of Persia, Darius III.

332 B.C. —— The Tyrians surrendered after seven months of fighting.

332 B.C. —— Alexander entered Egypt. He liberated them from Persian rule, and the Egyptians crowned him pharaoh.

331 B.C. —— Alexander founded Alexandria on the western edge of the Nile Delta.

331 B.C. —— Alexander made a trip through the Libyan Desert to the oasis of Siwah. There he consulted the Zeus-Ammon oracle. Alexander was pronounced the son of Zeus-Ammon by the oracle.

October 1, 331 B.C. —— Alexander left Egypt and traveled into the Persian Empire.

Winter 331-330 B.C. —— Alexander captured Babylon and Susa.

327 B.C. —— Alexander married Roxanne, a princess from Bactria.

326 B.C. —— Alexander's forces reached the upper Indus River Valley.

325 B.C. —— Alexander had ships built. Part of his army sailed westward from the mouth of the Indus River. Alexander led the rest of the troops across the Desert of Gedorsia. More than half of the forces died on the way.

323 B.C. —— Alexander became ill with a fever while at Babylon.

June 10, 323 B.C. —— Alexander died.

Alexander the Great

It is said that the universe fashions a man's reality according to his dreams. What dreams fill the mind of a man who is born to rule the world? What visions does the heart see when power never before known to man is in one's future? Alexander, son of King Philip of Macedonia, dreamed of greatness from the beginning of his life, and envisioned himself as a conquering hero as a very young man. The dreams of Alexander came to pass and the visions became reality. Alexander the Great remains one of the most fascinating characters in all of mankind's history, and stands out as the most successful in bringing his grandiose dreams to fruition as a result of personal bravery, mental flexibility and astuteness, and most of all, vision. He believed it would be so, and so it was. Let us go back to several hundred years before the Common Era, to the part of the world then known, and enter the dreamer's native environment. We'll visit his homeland before his birth, and follow from the very beginning the amazing accomplishments and victories as well as the follies of Alexander which changed the world forever.

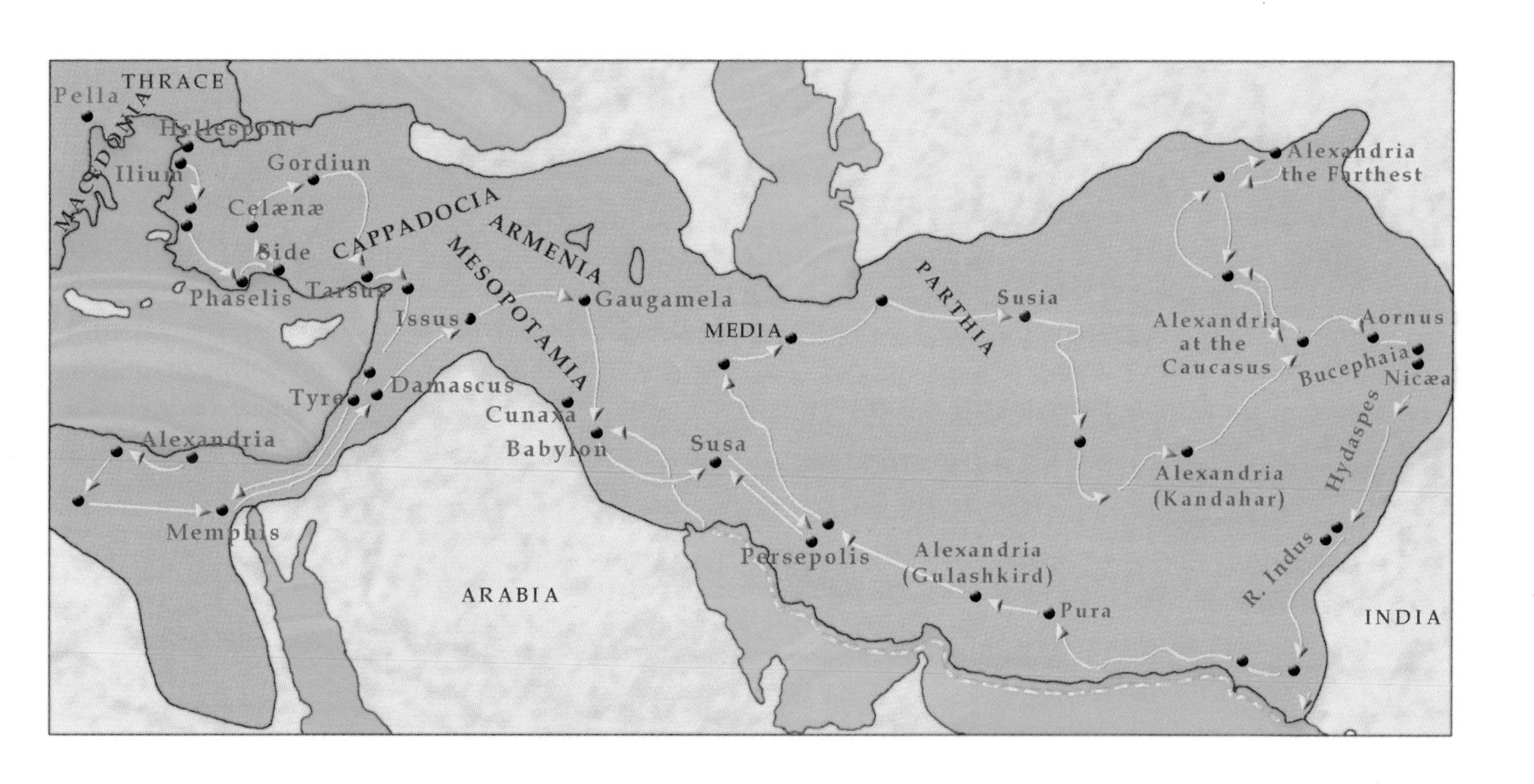
THRACE
Pella
MACEDONIA
Hellespont
Ilium
Gordiun
Celænæ
Side
Phaselis
Tarsus
CAPPADOCIA
ARMENIA
MESOPOTAMIA
Issus
Gaugamela
MEDIA
PARTHIA
Susia
Tyre
Damascus
Cunaxa
Babylon
Susa
Alexandria
Memphis
Persepolis
Alexandria
(Gulashkird)
Pura
ARABIA
Alexandria
the Farthest
Alexandria
at the
Caucasus
Aornus
Bucephaia
Nicæa
Alexandria
(Kandahar)
Hydaspes
R. Indus
INDIA

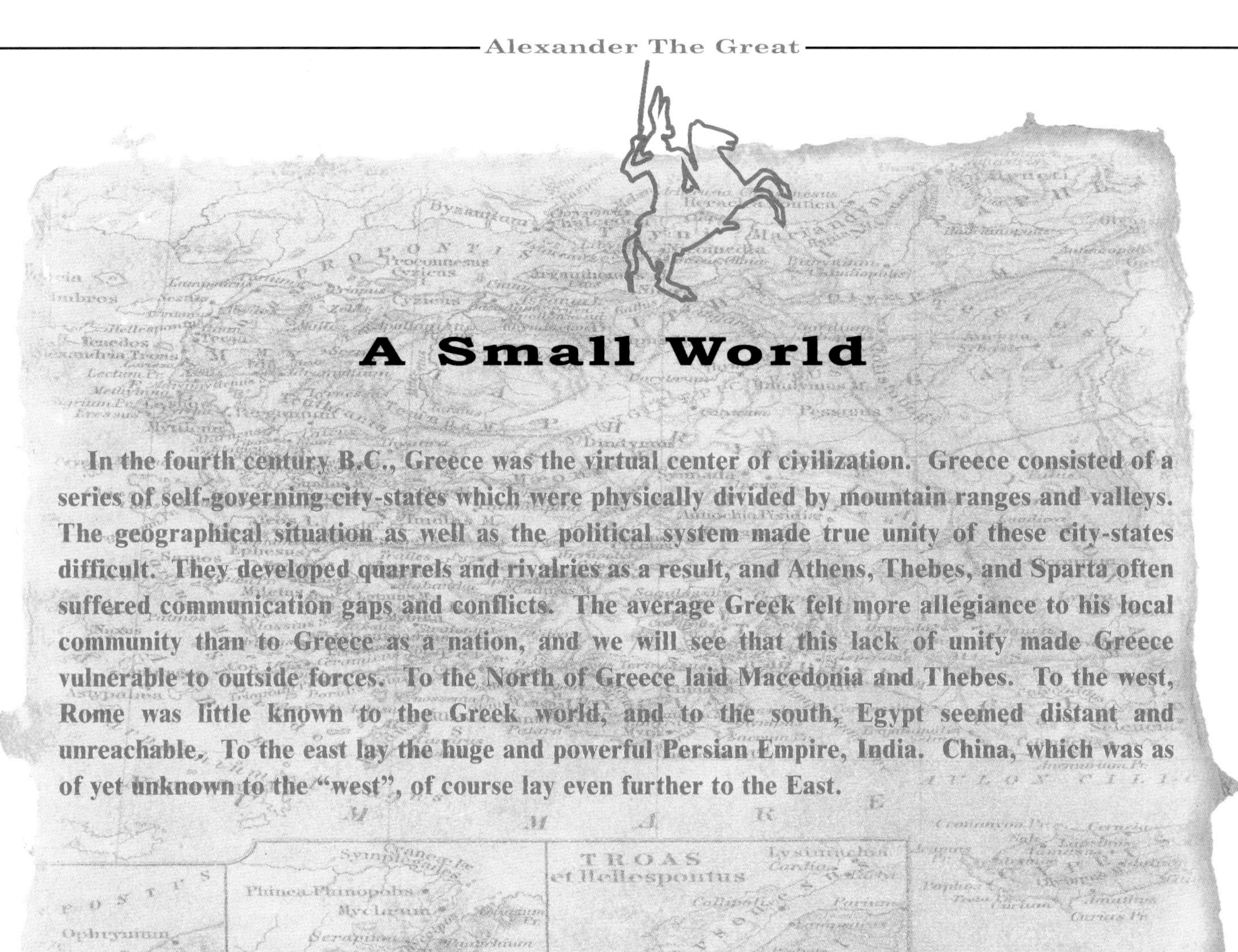

A Small World

In the fourth century B.C., Greece was the virtual center of civilization. Greece consisted of a series of self-governing city-states which were physically divided by mountain ranges and valleys. The geographical situation as well as the political system made true unity of these city-states difficult. They developed quarrels and rivalries as a result, and Athens, Thebes, and Sparta often suffered communication gaps and conflicts. The average Greek felt more allegiance to his local community than to Greece as a nation, and we will see that this lack of unity made Greece vulnerable to outside forces. To the North of Greece laid Macedonia and Thebes. To the west, Rome was little known to the Greek world, and to the south, Egypt seemed distant and unreachable. To the east lay the huge and powerful Persian Empire, India. China, which was as of yet unknown to the "west", of course lay even further to the East.

Greek culture was highly developed and had already brought forth minds which are spoken of still today with reverence. Pericles, the brilliant statesmen, Sophocles and Aristophanes, the great dramatists, and the historians Thucydides and Herodotus sprang from this unforgettably rich period for the development of human thought. Philosophers whose fame and influence are unmatched to this day – Socrates, Aristotle and Plato; Ancient Greece was a veritable goldmine of outstanding thinkers. It is a well-known and accepted fact the gifts of early Greek culture were phenomenal and affected the course of mankind's forever forward. The kernel of Democracy itself began to sprout roots and tendrils in this fertile environment.

The Greeks' Macedonian cousins to the north, on the other hand, did not excel in the arts or sciences, as they did not produce famous philosophers. Macedonia covered the territory where today lie Bulgaria, Yugoslavia, and Northern Greece. The Macedonian people were most likely descended from a mixed group of northern peoples, and were not closely related genetically to the Greeks. The Greeks denigrated the Macedonians, called them primitive and barbaric. Their habits and accents were ridiculed in every quarter in Greece. Even the fact that they still had a monarchy was considered base and uncivilized.

King Philip of Macedonia

In 359 B.C., King Philip II took over the throne of Macedonia after his brother, King Perdiccas III died in battle with the Illyrians. The actual heir to the Kingdom was Philip's infant nephew to whom he had been appointed regent, but Philip soon saw to it that the child was shunted aside, and assumed the Kingship himself at twenty three years of age.

Philip was an intelligent and educated youth in a society where few were literate. It is said that his mother was an unusual woman who taught herself to read at an advanced age and instilled in Philip the importance of study and knowledge. He was a stocky man with a full dark beard and thick dark curls. Wounded in early military campaigns, he was blinded in one eye, and was lame in one leg. He shunned royal robes and instead donned regular country clothes or covered himself in armor. He ruled with a fiery temper and headstrong will, but was an astute and wise politician who knew how to sway opinions and win respect.

Philip admired Greek culture and encouraged the Hellenization of his people. He even claimed to have descended from Greek ancestry, and spoke a common Greek dialect, albeit with a Macedonian accent. Members of his royal court were instructed to speak Greek as well. As a youngster, Philip was taught Greek politics and learned Greek military strategy. Although the Greeks at first called him Philip the Barbarian Philip would soon force his neighbors to the south to perceive him, and indeed Macedonia in a far different light than they that to which they had been accustomed.

King Philip II

Pella, the capital city of Macedonia, was the seat of Philip's Kingdom, and from there he ruled a country blessed with natural beauty and resources, just as it was rich in human resources. Agriculture was developing quickly and successfully and the energetic peoples of Macedonia were prospering from raising cattle and sheep and enjoying abundant fruit at harvest time. In addition, vast timber forests covered much of the land, and the Macedonians were fast turning these gifts into a sturdy economic base.

Philip was a driven man. He set goals and met them systematically and determinedly. He had a clear vision of Macedonia as a force which would soon rise and be reckoned with. He worked from an assumption that his calling was to fashion a powerful nation under his rule which would go forward and conquer the world. Philip's vision later became his son's vision, but without Philip's paving the way, undoubtedly the course of history would have been different. A man of action and clear objectives, not tired rhetoric, Philip not only desired power and glory for himself, but he wanted to form his nation as a united power that would change the face of the known world. Philip would often quote the Greek philosopher, Isocrates, who preached the unification of Greece as a sacred goal. Like Isocrates, Philip was annoyed by the constant bickering between the Greek city-states and firmly believed that unity must be restored at all costs. The city states had almost managed to destroy one another in the Peloponnesian war in the previous century and Philip considered this an enormous and unnecessary waste of human life and resources. His first and driving ambition was to unite Greece, doing away with separate states and in so doing to form a league with Greece and Macedonia. From that base, he wanted go on to annex all the neighboring countries, and indeed all of civilization. His ultimate objective was for the entire world to unite under him, King Philip of Macedon.

Pella ruins

The politically and militarily astute Philip instigated new policies which enhanced and unified his base of support and strengthened the country's ability to defend itself, and most importantly, to conquer. He bestowed nobility on his supporters and enlisted teenage boys into service, bringing a sense of national pride to the youngsters and their families.

The Macedonian army under King Philip grew to be extremely disciplined and professional, with a mighty cavalry such as the world had never before seen. Philip developed and introduced several brilliant new warfare strategies, including the infamous "phalanx". The infantry troops would line up close to one another, carrying long spears – over 4 meters in length. These soldiers would form a wall of men, shields, and spears, which advanced together as one piece. Combined with an infantry unit which also formed a wall of troops, the phalanx proved to be almost invincible, and worked its magic again and again in the Philip's campaigns, and later in Alexander's. Perhaps the most significant contribution made by Philip to the military world, however, was his establishment of a permanent standing army. Rather than gather up a rough army just before marching off to battle, Philip enlisted year-round troops who were constantly undergoing training and lived in military quarters supported by the state. Their training was extremely exacting and rigorous and the officers maintained a high standard of discipline. In a short time the Macedonian army became the best trained and equipped in the world.

By 358 B.C., Philip had succeeded in defeating the Illyrians, bringing safety and harmony back to Macedonia which had been defeated by the Illyrians during Philip's brother's reign. The Macedonian people rallied around Philip after this victory, and his Kingship was secure.

Two years after assuming the throne, at age twenty five, Philip traveled to the Island of Samothrace to attend a pagan festival which included various occult ceremonies and a gathering of oracles, witches, and members of Dionysian cults. At this event, Philip met a lovely princess from a small country called Epirus, which lay to the west of Macedonia, which is now modern Albania. Olympias, an intense, light-skinned young woman with auburn hair, was the daughter of the late King of Epirus, who was said to have descended directly from the legendary god Achilles, hero of Homer's Illiad. Her personality was strong and outgoing and her temper fierce and she was strikingly beautiful. Philip was charmed, and they developed affection for one another, which was followed while still in Samothrace by a marriage proposal. The pair returned together to Macedonia and had a royal wedding there.

Alexander is Born

Philip overlooked his new wife's deep fascination with the barbarous and demonic rites that were practiced at the festival, and only later realized that she brought such beliefs and behaviors to her daily life. At the beginning of their marriage Philip allowed himself to be influenced by his wife and soon he too was somewhat indoctrinated with the rites of Samothrace. The royal couple steeped themselves in the mysticism and symbolism of dreams and visions, and believed in signs and prophecies. Thus, when they discovered that Olympias was carrying their child, they sought out the oracles to interpret their various dreams. Olympias dreamt that her womb was struck by lightening, and Philip dreamt that he placed the seal of the lion on her belly. These dreams were deemed to mean that the child was destined to greatness, and that he would be invincible as the legendary god Ammon. It was prophesied that the child would bring about such changes in the world that a new era would be ushered in, changing human culture forever. Philip and Olympias would have been deeply shaken to know how very true the prophecy would prove to be.

Meanwhile, Philip had begun to carry out his plans to conquer and unify Greece. Using diplomacy when he could and brute military force when circumstances necessitated it. Philip invited the Greek city states to join him voluntarily and attempted to convince them of the benefits of unification under the Macedonian King. Many Greeks quite agreed with him and he had quite a following of loyal Greek citizens. Others, however, opposed him vehemently, fearing that Greek freedom was being challenged and jeopardized by the Macedonian upstart. Philip would not be deterred. He swept through Greece, forming alliances where he could, and fighting where words did not suffice.

In late July, 356 B.C., Philip was in Greece with his armies near Potidaea, where he had laid siege on a community which had risen in revolt. He would stay away until he had secured the territory for Macedonia. While he was at a meeting in his tent, a mounted courier who had made his way from Pella in search of the King rode up to the Macedonian camp bearing three important messages. The first announced that Philip's armies had been successful in the campaign in Illyria. The second message brought the welcome news that one of Philip's own horses had won a prize in an Olympic contest. The third message pleased Philip by far the most. Olympias had born him a healthy and robust son, and his name was Alexander.

Royal Childhood

Alexander was a fair and handsome child, sometimes with a ruddy cast to his skin. His hair was curly like his fathers, but finer and quite light in color. His eyes shown with intelligence and intensity like those of his mother.

Alexander's temperament closely matched that of both of his parents. All three possessed a strong will, and were impulsive and quick to anger. A taste for adventure and an insatiable curiosity about what lay just over the horizon also ran in the family. Even as a small boy, Alexander seemed to be impatient to begin his own career. He is noted to have expressed frustration whenever he was told of Philip's exploits and victories. He would often exclaim "but if my father conquers the world, what will be left for me to accomplish?" Already he dreamed of greatness and knew it awaited him just around the corner of adulthood. The young prince guarded his imperial countenance with great pride and refused to take part in the popular pursuits of his peers, like wrestling and boxing, although he enjoyed solitary sports such as hunting and distance running. Alexander never allowed himself to demonstrate fear and took physical risks without flinching. It was suggested to him that he consider competing at the Olympic Games in foot-racing, but he refused, saying it would be beneath him to compete against anyone but other Kings!

Although Philip was often away during Alexander's early childhood, the boy worshipped his father and treasured every moment he was allowed to be in his presence. Philip adored his son, and ensured that Alexander's education would be exemplary. He was determined to train his son to one day take his place as King, having no doubt that Alexander would inherit the rule of a large and powerful Macedonian empire, which he, Philip, would hand down to him as a result of his campaigns. Philip devoted serious thought and effort to making sure that Alexander would be ready for the enormous responsibilities this would entail. The King secured only the most illustrious teachers and instructors for the prince. Leonidas, a cousin of Olympias, was the first royal tutor. He trained Alexander to appreciate the virtues of an austere and Spartan way of life. This influence stayed with Alexander during his future years of tramping through desserts, when he would eat simply, sleep among his troops, and generally live an ascetic existence.

Life for a prince in the Macedonian court included some exposure to the arts, although it was not the main thrust of his education. When Alexander displayed an unusual talent for music, he was brought another teacher, Lysimachus, under whom he learned to play the harp and the lyre, and to appreciate other arts. Alexander enjoyed these pursuits, but Philip became concerned lest the boy be drawn too much toward artistic activities, and made sure that young Alexander spent equal time among the troops, observing and absorbing military behavior, discipline, and strategy. Even as a small boy, the prince was a regular visitor to the army barracks and strategy meetings of the officers.

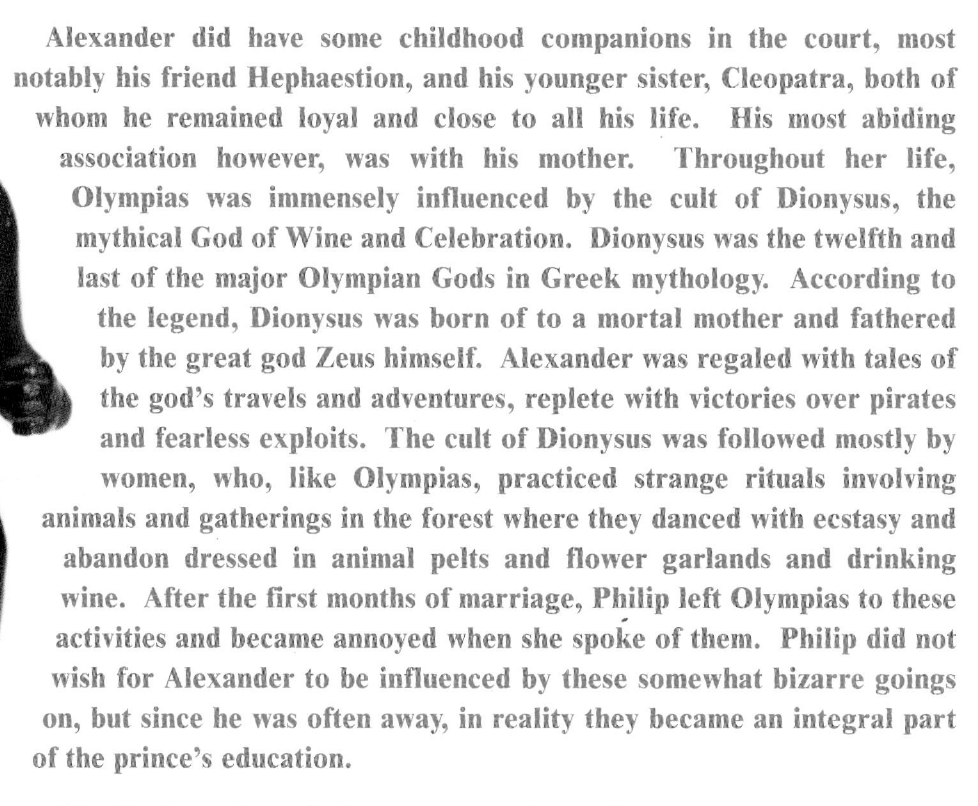

Alexander did have some childhood companions in the court, most notably his friend Hephaestion, and his younger sister, Cleopatra, both of whom he remained loyal and close to all his life. His most abiding association however, was with his mother. Throughout her life, Olympias was immensely influenced by the cult of Dionysus, the mythical God of Wine and Celebration. Dionysus was the twelfth and last of the major Olympian Gods in Greek mythology. According to the legend, Dionysus was born of to a mortal mother and fathered by the great god Zeus himself. Alexander was regaled with tales of the god's travels and adventures, replete with victories over pirates and fearless exploits. The cult of Dionysus was followed mostly by women, who, like Olympias, practiced strange rituals involving animals and gatherings in the forest where they danced with ecstasy and abandon dressed in animal pelts and flower garlands and drinking wine. After the first months of marriage, Philip left Olympias to these activities and became annoyed when she spoke of them. Philip did not wish for Alexander to be influenced by these somewhat bizarre goings on, but since he was often away, in reality they became an integral part of the prince's education.

Of all the tales of the youngest Olympian god, those that most completely captured the imagination of the young prince involved Dionysus' travels. The God of Wine and Celebration was said to have followed a long and fascinating route which led him to Egypt, India, and Persia, where he introduced the wonders of wine and wine-making to the natives and taught them to plant and harvest grapes. Later, Alexander's

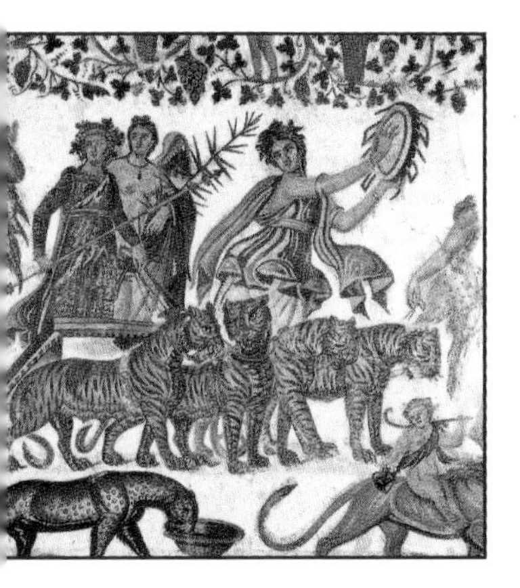

march to conquer the known world would follow roughly the same path as that of Dionysus, arriving at the faraway destinations in reverse order to the god's route.

Alexander's childhood existence straddled his parents' vastly different worlds. Part of his nature took happily to his mother's realm, while the larger portion of his interests lay in his father's. Alexander soaked in the atmosphere of great ideas, exciting changes, and ambitious plans which permeated Philip's court, and knew he was being bred for grandiose deeds and great ideas.

In 343 B.C., when the prince was 13 years old, Alexander's education took a momentous turn. The revered Greek scientist and thinker Aristotle was summoned to Pella to teach Alexander and the other children of the Macedonian aristocracy. Philip gladly paid him handsomely to be the prince's companion and mentor and Alexander blossomed intellectually under the great man's tutelage. He excelled in his studies, learning natural science and medicine, and discussing with Aristotle the fields of political thought and law. Aristotle drilled Alexander in the use of his reasoning powers and logical thought. He introduced him to the great literature of the time, and Homer's Iliad became Alexander's favorite book. Not only did he commit its text completely to memory – he even kept a copy under his pillow every night, along with his dagger, for many years. The images the book conjured of Greek heroism during the Trojan War powered his dreams. Alexander was quite devoted to Aristotle, and remained in touch with him throughout his life, providing his teacher with money for acquisition of books and to further his scientific inquiries. Alexander was quoted as saying during his later years, "My father gave me life, but Aristotle showed me how to live it".

Aristotle's home and birthplace was the town of Stagira, near the border of Greece and Macedonia. Several years before Aristotle came to Pella; Philip's armies had destroyed the town and exiled its citizens. Philip was proud of his son's relationship with the esteemed philosopher, and delighted with the way Alexander's education had unfolded, and no doubt felt a modicum of guilt over the fate of Aristotle's home city. The King had Stagira rebuilt and its inhabitants were allowed to return to their homes, as Philip's way of showing his appreciation for the tutor's influence on his son and heir.

Aristotle

As the years of Alexander's childhood unfolded, Philip continued to successfully bring the Greek city-states under his control. Using their state of non-unity and their many quarrels and conflicts to his advantage, Philip took the cities one by one, until he had acquired quite a large portion of Greece. In 355 B.C. Philip took possession of the Thracian town of Crenides, changing its name to Phillipi. The city of Methone, to the south of Pella was taken in 353 B.C., and Philip advanced southward past Mount Olympus into Thessaly. In the next four years he had taken Stagira, Amphipolis, and Chalcidice. In Thrace, the city of Amphipolis fell to Macedonia. Though the naval forces of Athens tried, they failed to win back the city from Philip. In Amphipolis he took possession of Mt. Pangaeus, which was the site of rich gold mines, ensuring that Philip's future campaigns would not lack for financial backing, and giving him the wherewithal to bribe rather than fight when this was possible. Some of the city-states continued to make war against one another, at times using their alliance with Macedonia to strengthen their fight against rival Greeks, but Philip continually used this to his advantage and fortified his league with every conflict.

In 351 B.C., a Greek orator called Demosthenes began to make a series of anti-Philip speeches, warning the Athenians than Philip was stealing their freedom. These speeches came to be known as "Philippics", and to this day a Philippic denotes a speech which vociferously denounces someone or something. The Philippics blasted the Macedonian leader for having no Greek blood in his veins, and belittled Macedonia as a primitive land of barbarians. In 348 B.C. the city-states tried again to unite, this time under Aeschines against Philip, but their campaign too was unsuccessful.

Between and during some of these battles, Philip did come home to Pella to see his son. On one notable occasion when Alexander was about 14 years old, Philip oversaw the delivery to his stables of a group of new horses which had been purchased for him. Among them was a gorgeous stallion named Bucephalus, which means "head of a bull". The jet-black horse

was enormous and uncommonly powerful. Philip's men had paid a huge sum for him, as he was truly exceptional animal. However, not one of the men was able to mount and ride Bucephalus. He raged and ran when approached, and bucked and reared like a wild beast when touched. Even human voices made the horse react with dangerous fury.

Alexander sat near his father and watched as the men tried and failed to mount the wondrous horse. The prince was moved and fascinated by the animal. Somehow the thought came to him that this fabulous beast would be his very own horse. When finally Philip despaired of their succeeding to break him, he ordered Bucephalus be returned to the market and their money refunded. When Alexander heard this he looked up at his father and begged him not to return the horse, promising that he himself would break the animal! Philip was incredulous that a mere boy, even his own son, could believe he would be successful at mounting a steed which even his most experienced cavalrymen had failed to approach, but Alexander's pleadings were incessant until Philip decided to give him a chance, under certain conditions. They made an agreement that Alexander would ride Bucephalus, or he would have to find a way to pay for him himself.

Unbeknownst to Philip or to anyone else at that point, Alexander possessed sharp, shrewd observational talents. He had watched carefully as the men tried to approach the horse. The prince had noticed something that had escaped the attention of everyone else present. He had seen that Bucephalus was afraid of his own shadow! Alexander agreed to Philip's terms, by which he would have to pay his father the huge sum of thirteen talents (equivalent today to tens of thousands of dollars) if he did not succeed in riding Bucephalus. To everyone's surprise, the boy strode calmly and confidently up to the horse. Quickly grabbing his bridle, he swung Bucephalus around so that he faced the sun. When he could no longer see his shadow jump and sway, Bucephalus slowly relaxed and became less agitated and frightened. When the horse bent his head for a split second, Alexander leaped onto his back, and within seconds they were cantering, then galloping, as if they had always been together. Philip was shocked and surprised and extremely proud of his son. By the time Alexander dismounted it was clear that Bucephalus was to be his horse and non other's. Alexander led Bucephalus back toward his father, and Philip, deeply moved by what he had witnessed, declared: "My son, Macedonia will be too small a Kingdom for you – you will have to find other worlds to conquer".

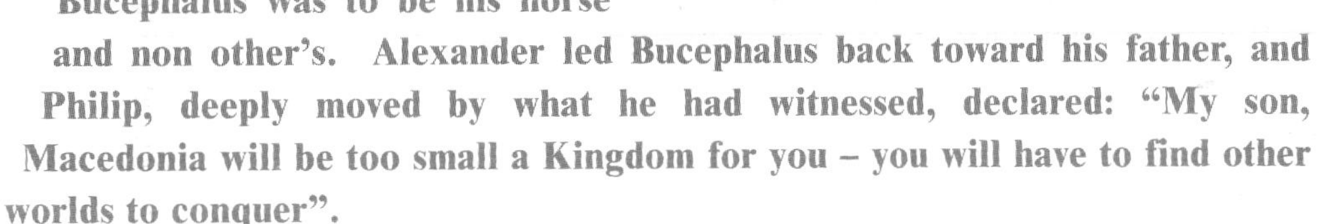

Bucephalus became Alexander's own steed, and the two were inseparable.

Bucephalus carried his master into every battle, until, when he became too old to do more than walk; Alexander would mount him only while he addressed his troops before a strike, and then transfer to a younger and stronger horse.

Alexander Comes of Age

When Alexander was sixteen years old Philip and his armies set off toward Thrace, where they laid siege on Perinthus and Byzantium. During this absence Philip for the first time ordered that his son the prince be left in charge of affairs in Macedonia. Alexander was left with full powers to act in his father's name as long as Philip was gone. It was a golden moment for Alexander to prove himself to his father, to the Macedonians, and to the world.

Philip did not make this decision lightly – he had seen to it that Alexander was thoroughly trained and felt he was ready for any eventuality.

Losing no time after Philip's departure, tribes from Maedi in Thrace almost immediately launched a rebellion. They apparently thought that the young and inexperienced prince would be no match for them, but in this they were sorely mistaken. Alexander rose quickly to the occasion and marched Macedonian troops bravely toward the rebels, crushing them and seizing their capital, and changing its name to Alexandropolis. It was a brilliant victory for the boy, and Philip was exceedingly proud and gratified.

The World According to Philip

Philip continued his successful campaign to conquer and unite Greece. He was victorious in battle after battle and deal after deal, until his Kingdom was the unquestioned dominant power. In 339 B.C. the Greek city-states Athens and Thebes were still warring one against the other. Philip had as yet not tried to subdue Athens, and decided it was an opportune time, while the Athenians were occupied with the Theban conflict. However, as Philip made his way down to central Greece with his forces, Athens and Thebes suddenly put aside their differences in order to unite in a fight against the Macedonians. The resultant battle - the Battle of Chaeronea - was long and brutal, and there were many casualties on all sides. Leading Philip's cavalry was none other then Prince Alexander, then eighteen years old, riding Bucephalus. The Athenians and Thebans greatly outnumbered the Macedonians, but Philip's phalanx, commanded by Alexander, proved unbeatable even against those odds. Philip employed some creative trickery, such as pretending to retreat and then using the element of surprise, and at the end of the hard-fought battle Philip was the clear and decisive winner. Philip, along with Alexander, had accomplished Philip's dream – Greece, which had never succeeded in becoming united herself, was now united and reorganized under Macedonian authority. The eighteen year old Alexander had made a major contribution to this conflict, proving himself an outstanding and courageous cavalry commander.

Athens was now finally under Macedonian control, but Philip did not raise a destructive arm against the city. Philip had always held a deep respect for the Athenians, and he sent Alexander to negotiate an alliance with them which all considered favorable. Hephaestion accompanied Alexander on this mission, proving an indispensable and dependable friend and advisor. Sparta was then offered a similar alliance, and when the Spartans refused, Philip destroyed Sparta forthwith.

Philip was declared Captain General of all Greece. He set up the city of Corinth as the seat of a representative council, which under a federal constitution would judge any issues which might arise. The city-state system in Greece was a thing of the past. Greece now consisted of alliances, under Macedonian rule. Philip's system left Greek liberty and self-rule intact, while assuring stability and loyalty to him.

Philip's dream was taking shape. He had set himself up as General of a united Greece and Macedonia. It seemed the time was right for the next stage of his dream to be realized. Philip was at last ready to move against the mighty Persian Empire. In 336 B.C. Philip declared war on Persia, and a force of ten thousand Macedonian and Greek troops began to move into Asia Minor to liberate the Greek cities which were under Persian domination. Using naval power from Athens along with other armies from his league, Philip began to thrust eastward. He succeeded in bringing some Greek cities in Asia Minor into his league, and formed a buffer against Persia.

The End of Innocence

It was about this time that the good relations between Philip and his son began to become more complicated. Alexander was very close to his mother, Olympias, and the latter was very protective of her son and his position in the Macedonian court. Relations between Philip and Olympias however, were strained, and only became worse as the prince got older. Olympias had always been a sullen, even morose wife to Philip and often displayed an extremely jealous and suspicious nature. Polygamy was allowed in the Macedonian court, and Olympias was not Philip's first or only wife, although she was the only one named Queen of Macedonia. Olympias clashed with the lesser wives and tried to undermine them in any fashion that she could. When one of them gave birth to a mentally retarded infant, it was rumored that Olympias had deliberately poisoned the woman during her pregnancy, causing the defect. In addition, as time wore on, Philip became less tolerant of the Queen's preoccupation with Dionysian and Orphic cults. Some of her habits, such as allowing snakes to roam freely in their bedroom, angered and annoyed Philip, but even the King himself could not turn Olympias from her strange behaviors. By the time Alexander reached 17 years of age, his parents were quite estranged. Some attribute their differences to the gaps in their cultures, and the fact that Olympias was not a native Macedonian. Others point out the fact that Olympias was a difficult, intense, and jealous woman who drove Philip away with her possessiveness and quirky practices. There can be little doubt that Philip's taking an additional wife at this time could only have fueled jealousies and resentment, and was a turning point for the entire family. Although Philip reportedly wed a total of seven wives in his lifetime, his last wedding was particularly irksome to Olympias, and she perceived it as a serious threat to her own stand, as well as to Alexander's. It seemed to be an attempt to provide the Kingdom with additional heirs who might someday be able to compete with Alexander for the throne. She was wild with jealousy when Philip announced his engagement, and regaled Alexander with her insinuations, trying, apparently with some success, to instigate her son against his father.

Philip had chosen Cleopatra, a young Macedonian woman, as his bride in the year 337 B.C. Cleopatra's uncle and legal guardian, Attalus, was an outspoken man who despised Olympias and regarded Alexander a bastard as a result of his "impure" breeding. There was even talk of Attalus himself trying to grab the Macedonian throne. After the wedding ceremony, Attalus chose the occasion of the reception to become drunk on wine and to shout provocative and insulting jibes at Alexander. Standing to make a toast to the newlyweds, he cried out that now that a member of his pure Macedonian family was wed to the King, a suitable heir would soon be born to Philip, so that Alexander, with his non-Macedonian blood, would become an unnecessary appendage to the family.

olympias

Hearing this, Alexander's impulsive temper came to the fore and he angrily rose and addressed the drunken speaker: "I am the LAWFUL heir!" he shouted, and threw his heavy metal cup, striking Attalus in the head. Attalus collapsed as a result of the blow. Philip, who was in quite a drunken state, rose and drew his sword in reaction to this ruckus. The King was so inebriated that he was unable to take more than a few steps away from his table before he fell forward onto the floor. We shall never know whom Philip had meant to attack – Attalus for insulting his son, or Alexander for his outburst. Alexander strode over to his father and standing jeeringly over the prostrate King he shouted to the crowd: "Behold my father, the man who says he will cross the straits into Asia but who cannot even manage to cross from one table to another!"

Alexander's attack on his father in public in this manner was more than impudent. Many feared the Philip would inflict a severe punishment on his son for such behavior. Indeed, this event was a turning point in the relations between father and son, and everything changed between them. This was apparently according to Alexander's wishes, however, and not Philip's, for although he had been humiliated by his son, Philip tried desperately to win back Alexander's affection. Olympias' indelible influence however, seemed to have permeated Alexander's attitudes and he never softened his stance nor reconciled completely with Philip. Olympia even began to refer to Alexander as the son of the god Apollo, and not Philip's son at all. Philip divorced Olympias soon after the incident at the wedding, and she left Macedonia, perhaps because she was exiled by Philip or perhaps she wished to distance herself by choice. Alexander fled Macedonia along with his mother for a time, out of loyalty, but he could not shake his longing to be in the thick of things, and soon responded to his father's pleas that he return to the court in Pella. Though he resumed his role of crown prince and heir, the relations between father and son remained cool and aloof.

To make matters worse, from her perch in exile, Olympias managed to further fuel nineteen year old Alexander's resentments of his father. Philip had received an offer to wed another of his sons, Alexander's half brother from a marriage previous to Olympias, to a princess from Caria in Asia Minor. Although the older prince was known to be of limited mental capacity, and no threat to Alexander's future Kingship, Olympias chose to make an issue of the princess having been offered to him rather than to her son, and encouraged Alexander to suspect his father of trying to undermine him. Behind Philip's back, and at his mother's urging, Alexander sent a message to the princess's father offering his own hand in marriage in place of his brother's. Philip was torn apart with pain that Alexander could believe he'd tried to undercut him, or that the marriage would in any way threaten him. Alexander's impetuous act angered the King, and he finally let loose his own temper on his son, telling him he deserved whatever befell him if he could be so thick-headed as to offer himself to a barbarian Asian princess! Alexander reneged on his offer of marriage but remained aloof and suspicious where Philip was concerned.

The King is Dead – Long Live the King

In July of 336 B.C. Philip celebrated his twentieth birthday. His childhood had long since been over, and he'd been groomed for some time to take over the Kingdom, but he could not have known or guessed that it would happen so soon.

Philip returned from Asia that summer to attend the wedding of his daughter Cleopatra, Alexander's sister. Cleopatra was to marry their uncle, Olympias' brother, the King of Epirus. Philip planned a huge celebration to which he invited many Greek dignitaries and arranged an impressive musical and theatrical presentation. The opening ceremony was to take place in a theater, and as the guests assembled, Philip himself appeared with his guards and walked toward the entrance. Waiting for him in the shadows near the theater door was Pausanias, a member of Philip's court who had served in his bodyguard. Pausanias had a grievance against Philip and his Kingship. He felt he had been ignored by Philip when he complained of mistreatment at the hands of Cleopatra's uncle, Attalus. As Philip passed by him toward the entrance, Pausanias leapt forward and stabbed the King several times in the back. Philip died immediately without a struggle, and no last words have been recorded in history. The assassin tried to escape, but Philip's guards gave chase and immediately put him to death as well. As might be expected, rumors flew that Olympias was the designer of the assassination plot, and there were claims that even Alexander may have had a hand in his father's demise, but these were neither substantiated nor disproved.

The greatest King the world had yet known was gone. Philip's many accomplishments laid a firm groundwork for his estranged but beloved son to take over, and his numerous important contributions to military and political strategy were considerable. If Alexander had not gone on to become such a momentous figure in his own right, Philip's name would perhaps have lived on as the greatest King in history.

There was a short period of confusion during which several other contenders for the throne made themselves known. Alexander's cousin, Amyntas, whose Kingship had been usurped by Philip when Amyntas was a toddler, made a brief play for the throne. Alexander lost no time having him and other minor would-be Kings executed. He also promptly rounded up his father's assassin and his accomplices and punished them.

Olympia also went into a frenzy of activity. She was determined that nothing and no-one would stand in the way of Alexander taking over his father's throne, and she saw a clear path to doing away with those toward whom she had for years held resentments and jealousies. So it was that one after another, Philip's various other wives and mistresses were slaughtered along with their children, including of course, Cleopatra and her tiny daughter. The death of Cleopatra extinguished any hopes that her uncle may have had of making a play for the throne himself. Alexander, however, severely reprimanded his mother for the murders of his stepmother and tiny sister, deeming them brutal, and in any case, unnecessary.

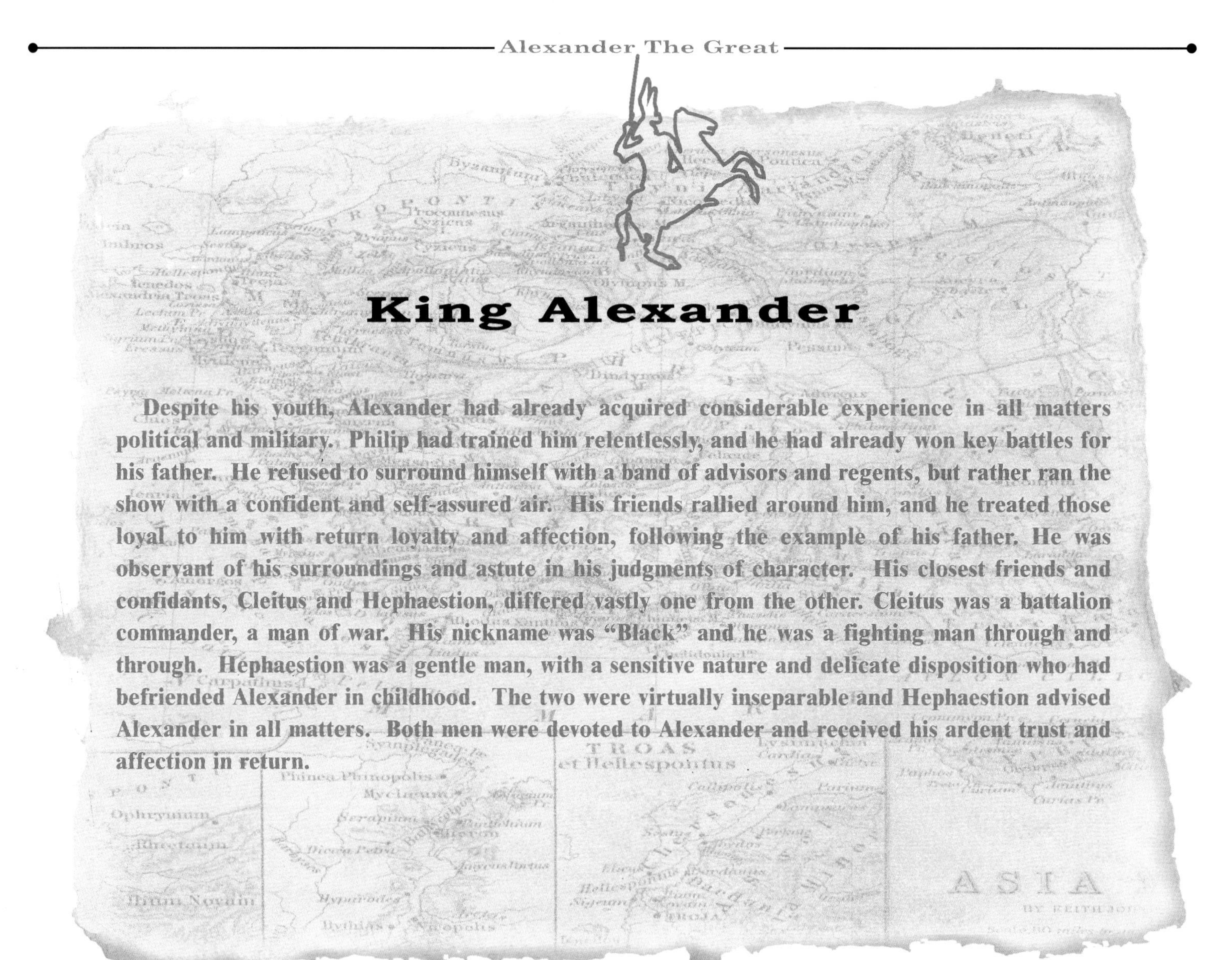

King Alexander

Despite his youth, Alexander had already acquired considerable experience in all matters political and military. Philip had trained him relentlessly, and he had already won key battles for his father. He refused to surround himself with a band of advisors and regents, but rather ran the show with a confident and self-assured air. His friends rallied around him, and he treated those loyal to him with return loyalty and affection, following the example of his father. He was observant of his surroundings and astute in his judgments of character. His closest friends and confidants, Cleitus and Hephaestion, differed vastly one from the other. Cleitus was a battalion commander, a man of war. His nickname was "Black" and he was a fighting man through and through. Hephaestion was a gentle man, with a sensitive nature and delicate disposition who had befriended Alexander in childhood. The two were virtually inseparable and Hephaestion advised Alexander in all matters. Both men were devoted to Alexander and received his ardent trust and affection in return.

Physically, Alexander was an imposing and handsome figure of medium height and size. He possessed of a natural vigor and strength which was guarded with frequent exercise and moderate diet. He was not a man of particular excess with drink, although drinking large amounts on occasion was certainly acceptable in the Macedonian world. Alexander was a vain man, but not narcissistic. His vanity is apparent from the tremendous number of portraits, coins, and medals which bore his likeness. From these, we know that he was clean-shaven (in an age when virtually all men wore beards) and had thick hair upswept from his forehead.

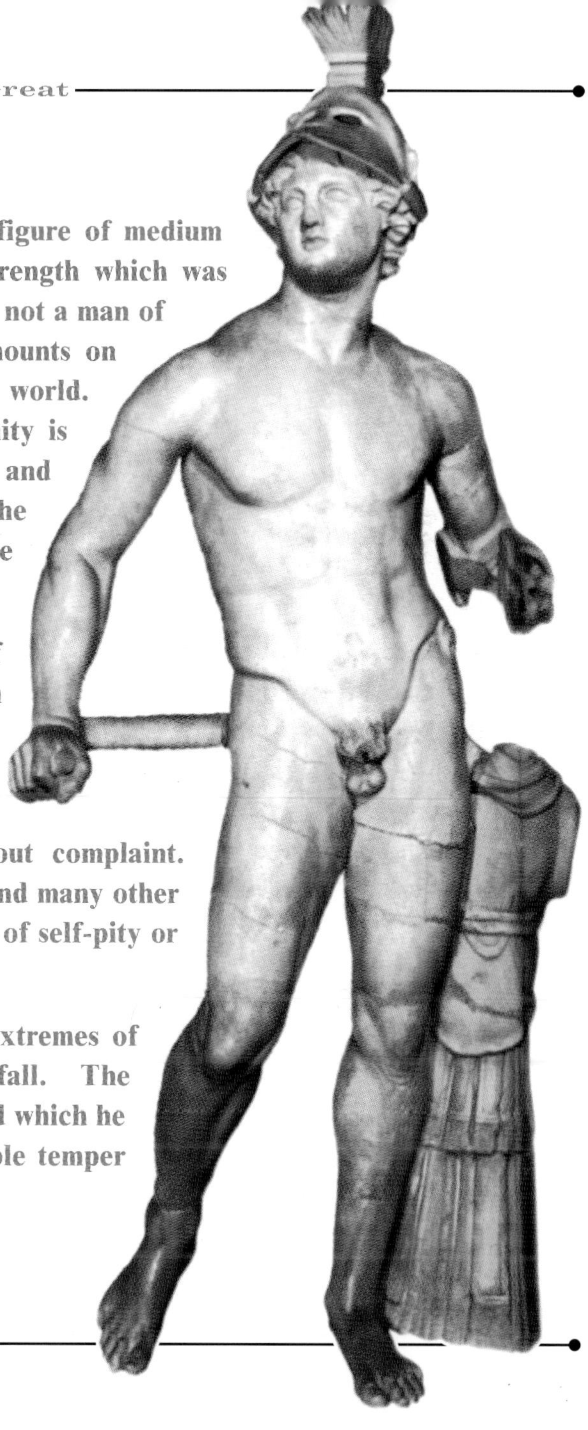

The young King was inspired by a curious amalgam of influences. His characteristics and aspirations sprang from his devotion to Dionysus as a god, Achilles as a hero, and the Homer's Illiad as his manual of warfare. Alexander was not afraid of physical pain or hardship, and would endure all manner of personal deprivation and affliction without complaint. Hunger and thirst, extremes of weather and temperature, and many other forms of suffering were endured by the King with no trace of self-pity or anguish.

His personality was complex, and as we will see, the extremes of which he was capable would ultimately prove his downfall. The gentleness and tenderness of which he was quite capable and which he demonstrated often coexisted with a fiery and unpredictable temper and even an ability to be cruel at times.

Across the Mighty Danube

News of Philip's death soon reached the far corners of the Greek and Macedonian territory, and reactions began to be felt in various quarters. Many Greeks considered Alexander a mere inexperienced youth who could easily be duped and disposed of. We have to wonder how they managed so soon to forget his amazing performance at Chaeronea! Unrest and possible rebellion were in the air. Alexander traveled directly to Corinth where he quickly secured an interim agreement from the Greek states, in return for granting them local freedom. The council gave him a full mandate to fight for the Macedonian-Greek league against the Persian Empire, exactly as they had commissioned Philip to do. Alexander left Corinth as Captain General. The Greek collective memory retained great resentment against the Persians for their invasion of Greece over one hundred years before, and most of the Greeks stood behind Alexander's desire to rout out the Persian Empire. And this he certainly intended to do.

The new King knew, however, that before he began the Persian campaign there were other matters to attend to. Having bought himself time and general agreement from the Greeks, Alexander set out to take care of what he considered a most pressing task. Before setting out to make war against Persia, Alexander felt he must immediately assure his lines of supply and

communication from the north. Meanwhile, there too, there were threats of uprisings, and news of the northern people's plans to make some trouble had reached him. A secure northern base was essential before he set off for the east. So the Macedonian armies headed northward, into the savage wilderness, where tribe after hostile tribe awaited them. It was early in the year 335 B.C. when Alexander marched toward Thrace.

After a ten day march, Alexander and his men came upon a force of Thracian natives that had assembled above them on a mountain slope. The Thracians had organized a planned offensive consisting of wagons perched at the top of the high ground, aimed at the Macedonians below. There was no way around this predicament and no other path to the crest, so Alexander had to employ a creative solution. He ordered his men to lie down prone on the slope with their shields on their backs, pressed one against the other to form a road of shields for the wagons to pass over. The plan was a success – Alexander's men followed his orders and there were no casualties. The Thracian wagons caused a fearful commotion as they sped over the Macedonian soldiers, but after the wagons had careened down the mountain causing no harm, the men gathered their wits and Alexander ordered them to charge up the hill. The Thracian forces were so surprised at the failure of their plan, they were unable to mount serious resistance, and the Thrace fell into Alexander's hands. Many Thracians escaped on foot, some were taken captive, and about fifteen hundred were killed.

Alexander then pushed his army onward toward the Triballian camp. After a short battle in which the Macedonian cavalry stampeded the Triballians, Alexander was victorious, having killed thousands and sustaining only light casualties to his own army.

Three days later Alexander's men reached the mighty Danube. There, the Macedonian warships which had come up to meet them were waiting. Alexander took stock of the men and supplies on the ship, and his armies boarded. They set sail immediately for a large river island on which Thracians and Triballians had taken refuge. They made excellent time in reaching the island, but as the ships tried to land the weather shifted and swift currents prevented them from approaching the steep shore. Alexander assessed the situation on the island as too dangerous, and the ships gave up trying to land. Instead, they were ordered to make a daring push across the river to the far bank, where the Getae dwelled. The Getae had already amassed an army, ready to resist the Macedonians, and Alexander likely saw this situation as more pressing, in addition to the problems the ships were experiencing at the island.

Alexander crossed the Danube with around 1500 cavalry and 4000 infantry troops. They sailed all night, and landed just before dawn. The cavalry came ashore straight away, formed the traditional Macedonian phalanx, and advanced toward the Getae. The latter were already at a decided psychological disadvantage. After having witnessed the swift and surprising crossing of the river by the Macedonians, the advance of the phalanx shook their courage, and they fled, with Alexander's men in pursuit. The Getae rushed desperately back to their town, gathered up as their belongings and families, and fled onward as far inland as they could mange. When Alexander reached the town, it was deserted. The Macedonians plundered and burned the town, destroying it completely.

Several of the northern tribes, including the Triballians and the Celts, sent messages of peace and friendship to Alexander, undoubtedly wishing to avoid the fate of the Getae. The story goes that Alexander asked the Celtic envoy what he and his people feared most on the world, assuming that the answer would be "you, sir". He was disappointed when the answer came "We fear that the sky might fall onto our heads!" Alexander nevertheless made agreements of alliance with them before moving on to the area of the Agrianes, the Autairates, and the Taulantians.

King Lagarios of the Agrianes greatly admired Alexander, and sent him a message offering help of any sort, including an offer to attack the Autariates with his own troops, thus sparing the Macedonians the trouble. He in fact did so, causing much damage to the Autariates, who in any case were not a terribly warlike people and would have given Alexander's men little challenge. Nevertheless, Alexander did not let these services go without notice, and Lagarios received high honors and gifts from the Macedonian court. Alexander even went so far as to offer Lagarios his half-sister's hand in marriage, should Lagarios come to Pella to claim her. This sister was the daughter of Philip and one of his several wives. However, before the wedding could take place, Lagarios fell ill and died.

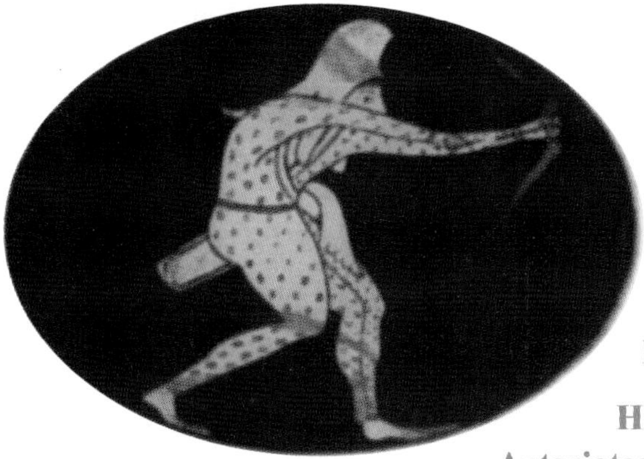

Having thus befriended the Agrianes, who dealt with the Autariates, Alexander had still to solve the problem of Cleitus, who was determined to revolt against the Macedonians. Cleitus had occupied a river town called Pelium, to which Alexander now pointed his ships. When they arrived, they lost no time mounting an attack. Cleitus' forces abandoned their positions almost the very moment they saw the Macedonians coming toward them. They retreated into their town, and Alexander shut them up in it and set up a blockade. Glaucias, Prince of the Taulantians, arrived the next day with the intention of reinforcing Cleitus. Considerable fighting then did take place, but after three days Cleitus' and Glaucias' men were becoming careless. Exhausted, they had set up camp without proper guards, and Alexander took proper notice and advantage. The Macedonians surprised the enemy in their tents asleep, and killed or captured them all, leaving no possibility for escape.

Alexander and his army made their way southward, weary but undefeated. The northern campaigns had accomplished much in a very short span of time.

Thebes Revolts

Alexander scarcely had time to revel in his victories in the north before he turned his attention back to Greece. While his attention had been devoted to the north, much had transpired which now caused Alexander concern. A rumor had circulated in Greece to the effect that Alexander had been killed. This rumor had been eagerly passed along, giving several prominent orators the audacity to resurrect the Philippics of Demosthenes and to again preach Greek freedom and liberty, calling for resistance to Macedonian rule. Many Greeks rallied around these sentiments, and they gained a respectable following. By the autumn of 335 B.C. the mood in Thebes had heated up to the point of threatened revolt. Alexander, upon hearing that the Philippics were again being heard in the Greek squares and forums, declared that Demosthenes would soon see that he had been but a boy in Illyria, and a youth in Thessaly, but that when he reached the walls of Thebes and Athens the Greeks would behold him in all his manhood. He soon made good on this promise in full.

Alexander moved a large force southward toward Thebes, and amassed his artillery outside the city gates. While emotions ran high in Thebes and motivation was strong to overthrow the Macedonians, many were impressed with what Alexander had accomplished in such a short time in the north, and a bit taken aback by his "return" to the living! As the Macedonians gathered at the gates of Thebes, the Theban rhetoric heated up, and the political rabble rousers gave boisterous and unceasing voice to the call for Greek liberty.

Before giving the signal to attack, Alexander gave the Thebans an opportunity to back down, sending in a message offering full forgiveness in return for surrender and the turning over of the ring-leaders of the intended revolt. The Thebans were by this time aching for a fight however, and sent a counter-offer which demanded that Antipater and Philotas, Alexander's trusted aids and advisors whom the Greeks despised, be killed. This was of course out of the question, and Alexander quickly lost his patience. He sounded the alarm, and his general, Perdiccas, attacked the gates of the Thebes. Once they had penetrated, the rest of the Macedonian force followed. The Thebans fought mightily and with a strong will, and the battle was difficult, but the Thebans were outnumbered and outmaneuvered by the Macedonians, and soon the city was overrun. In the days that followed the battle Thebes was thoroughly plundered, destroyed, and burned to the ground. While the Macedonians had captured the town, it was the Phocians, Plataeans, and others from neighboring towns, taking advantage of the Macedonian attack and seeing an opportunity to settle their scores with Thebes behaved with particular cruelty. They burst into Thebes and routed the people from their homes, murdering entire families -women, children, and elderly alike.

When silence finally fell at the end of the massacre and the horrors subsided, Thebes had entirely ceased to exist. Only the temples eerily rose from among the ashes, along with the home of one man, the poet Pindar, whose work Alexander greatly admired and had ordered spared along with members of his family.

In all, over six thousand were killed, and more taken into custody by Alexander's men.

It is here, at the beginning of Alexander's career as a conqueror that we begin to see the contradictory sides to his nature. He preferred to win by negotiation and alliance rather than with military might, but he would not shirk from "teaching a lesson" to any group that dared defy him. While he would brook no foe and never allowed himself a defeat, he had a softer side, and even harbored some guilty feelings over the suffering he caused the vanquished. The story is told that after the destruction of Thebes, Alexander's soldiers brought a woman prisoner before him for punishment. During the plundering of the city a Macedonian Captain forced her from her home and asked her where she hid her gold. She led him to her well behind her house and told him to look deep inside it. When he leaned over the well to have a look, she pushed him in, and killed him by dropping boulders into the well after him. When Alexander interrogated the woman she explained that not only had she killed his captain, but her brother had been an influential Theban who preached liberty for the

Greeks and had died fighting against his father, Philip. Alexander listened carefully to the woman's story, and after considering briefly, ordered her and her family set free. He declared her a woman of valor and bravery, which he deeply respected, even among his enemies. The guilt over what happened at Thebes never entirely left Alexander, and through the years whenever he met a former Theban he tried to treat him with special kindness.

Alexander had a basic liking for people and an ability to see them and appreciate them for their positive qualities, whether they were enemies or friends. Just after Philip's death when Alexander appeared before the Corinth council, many of the most respected and influential Greeks in the area had made their way to Corinth to be in the presence of the Macedonian King. Among them were philosophers and statesmen, and scholars of every discipline. Noticeably absent from their number was a philosopher called Diogenes of Sinope. Diogenes would have been expected to appear in Corinth to pay his respects to Alexander, but instead, he purposely ignored the King's presence in the vicinity, and went about his daily routine, including an afternoon sunbath in the backyard of his home just outside Corinth. Alexander decided that if Diogenes did not come to him, he would pay him a visit himself, and set out on foot for the philosopher's home. As Diogenes saw the King approaching with a crowd of people surrounding him, he remained supine on his couch, raised himself leisurely on an elbow and looked straight at Alexander, without so much as rising to greet him. Alexander asked the philosopher if there was anything he needed from the King, and the reply came: "Please, move over a bit as you are blocking the sun". Rather than be indignant or angry, Alexander was impressed with the pluck of

Diogenes and his ability to condescend even to a powerful King. As they departed, members of assembled company mocked and criticized the philosopher, but Alexander stopped them, declaring: "Say what you will, but if I were not Alexander, I would choose to be Diogenes".

The Greeks were shocked and horrified by the fate of their holy city of Thebes. The horrible example was not lost on them that Alexander was not to be confronted. Athens, too, had threatened to abandon the Macedonian alliance, but after what happened to Thebes, the Athenians reconsidered and backed down. Alexander had a mass of grievances against Athens and could have taken the city regardless, but perhaps he was sated with bloodshed for the time being and wished not to repeat the horrors of Thebes. Alexander paid a visit to Athens and a pact was sealed under which the situation in Athens remained as it had been under Philip. The Greek world had learned its lesson well, and remained firmly under Alexander until the end of his days.

Prophecy

Alexander was influenced by Olympias' belief in oracles and prophecies. Olympias had also impressed upon him that he was godlike man, perhaps descended from the deities themselves. He knew that the Greeks and Macedonians were as a whole quite a superstitious culture, and that many put great store in prophecies. On his return journey from Athens, Alexander paid a visit to the sacred city of Delphi, where he went to the Oracle of Delphi, in order to request a priestess to tell his future. Delphi was thought of as the "center of the universe", where cosmic energies were most potent, and it was believed that the god Apollo himself made Delphi his home. The King hoped for a favorable reading which would become known far and wide, thus giving him even a greater base of support and belief among the religious and superstitious Greek and Macedonian people.

Alexander and his entourage happened to arrive on an inauspicious day when the telling of fortunes was forbidden, and the priestess tried to refuse his demand for a prophecy. The King would have nothing of this, and gave the order to have her brought out against her wishes. When the priestess was forcibly made to appear before the oracle she had already been duly impressed by Alexander's might and fortitude. Under duress, she pronounced him "invincible", even before requesting a prophecy from the oracle. This was, of course, exactly what the young King had hoped to hear, and declaring he had heard enough, he left satisfied.

On another occasion early in Alexander's reign, a wooden statue of Orpheus was seen covered in "sweat". Many were alarmed at this omen, and worried that it was a portent of disaster to come. Alexander called for his most trusted soothsayer, Aristander, and asked for his interpretation of the sign. Aristander told the kind to take heart, for the sweat of Orpheus meant only that Alexander would cause poets and musicians to sweat under the effort of singing and playing in praise of his glory.

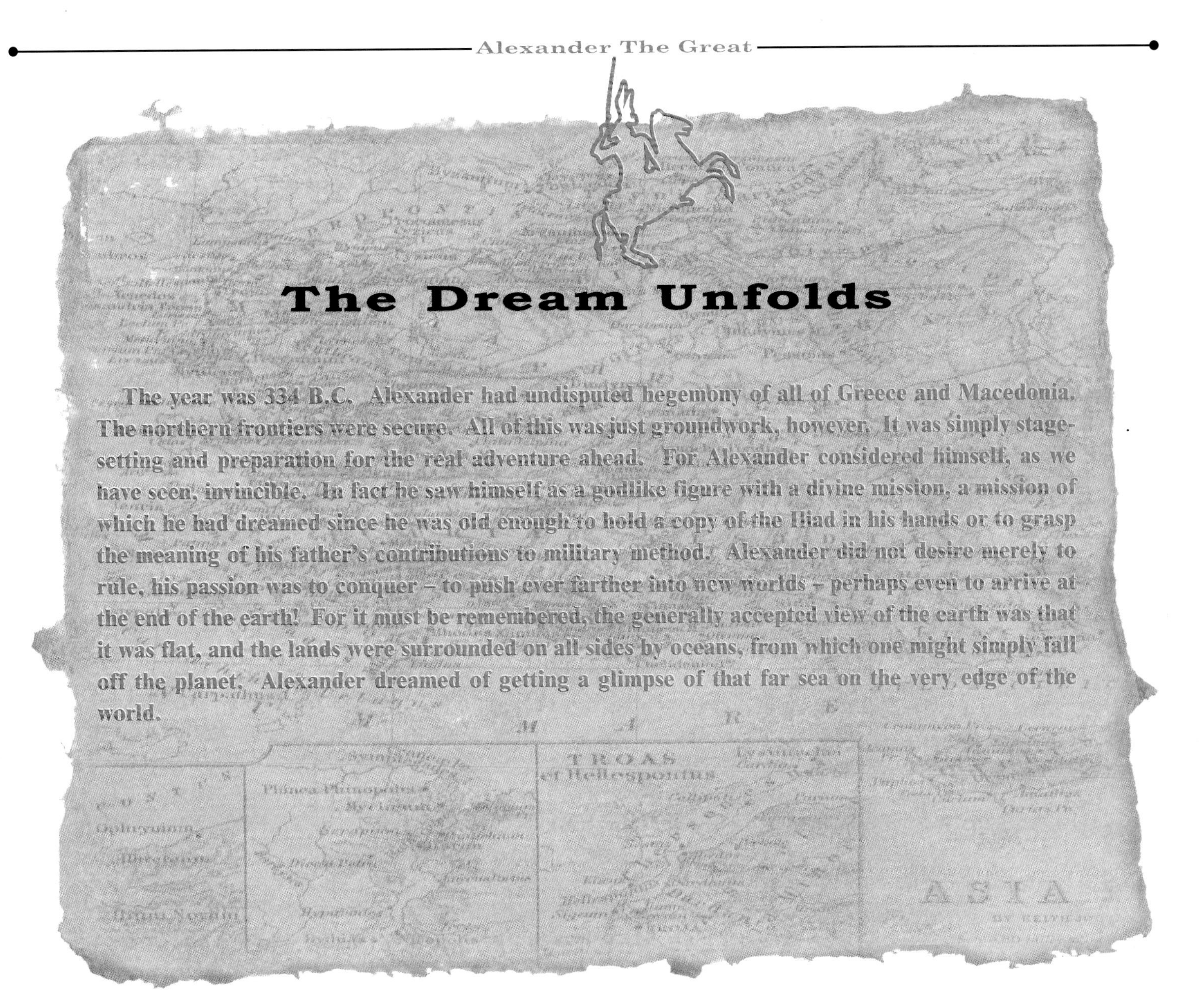

The Dream Unfolds

The year was 334 B.C. Alexander had undisputed hegemony of all of Greece and Macedonia. The northern frontiers were secure. All of this was just groundwork, however. It was simply stage-setting and preparation for the real adventure ahead. For Alexander considered himself, as we have seen, invincible. In fact he saw himself as a godlike figure with a divine mission, a mission of which he had dreamed since he was old enough to hold a copy of the Iliad in his hands or to grasp the meaning of his father's contributions to military method. Alexander did not desire merely to rule, his passion was to conquer – to push ever farther into new worlds – perhaps even to arrive at the end of the earth! For it must be remembered, the generally accepted view of the earth was that it was flat, and the lands were surrounded on all sides by oceans, from which one might simply fall off the planet. Alexander dreamed of getting a glimpse of that far sea on the very edge of the world.

Alexander was a man of high ideals, which must be respected against the backdrop of the culture of his time. He believed that he and his Pan-Hellenic armies of Greeks and Macedonians had a mandate to wipe out the tyranny which was suffered by so many of the world's population under the Persian Empire. He saw the Empire as evil and oppressive and aspired to rid the world of its influence as a moral imperative.

There can be little doubt that Alexander placed great importance on the stories of the deities on which he was weaned, just as we can be certain that he believed his mother when she told him he was descended from Hercules. Achilles, Alexander's greatest hero, was never far from his mind as a role model. The Trojan War was constantly replayed in his mind, and his longing to repeat or surpass the legendary victories was fierce.

Alexander gave very little thought, if any, to the possibility of defeat, and for many years reality gave way to his desires just as paint on canvas takes the form of a living thing which began as the artist's vision. He dreamed of one united world, under Macedonia, and held this as his ultimate goal.

Preparing to Meet the Persian Foe

The Persian Empire was ruled by King Darius III, a man forty-six years of age and past his personal prime, who was known in the Persian world as the King of Kings. Darius' vast dominion stretched from the Greek colonies of Asia Minor all the way to the borders of India. Darius' grandfather, King Darius the first, had extended the Persian Empire to such lengths that it was over a hundred times the expanse of the Macedonian-Greek territory. Xerxes, the next King of Persia, was remembered by the Greeks as the constant combatant who threatened and fought them continuously until his murder in 465 B.C. After Xerxes, the Persians ceased to attack Greece, but resentment and hatred did not subside. The Greeks despised the Persians and considered them dangerous savages and barbarians, although in reality Persian culture was quite refined and Persian commerce and arts were very notable and thriving.

Alexander's declared Darius III his mortal enemy. It was known that Darius was himself an intelligent and prudent King, but that his military forces and strategy were wanting. Nevertheless, what he may have lacked in military knowledge he tried to make up for in sheer numbers. Darius maintained a gigantic army which could certainly not be dismissed outright.

Alexander's Army

Throughout the summer and autumn of 335 B.C. Alexander's armies trained and prepared for the crossing into Asia. The Pan-Hellenist army under the twenty-two year old King consisted of over forty thousand troops. Of these, approximately seven thousand were forces sent by the Greek League allies. The over five thousand cavalry were drilled to precision and fitness, and the infantry were of the finest ever raised by the Macedonian army.

Alexander had inherited from Philip several vital military innovations. The Macedonian army consisted of several divisions. Approximately two thousand nobleman and lords, dubbed the "King's Companions" maneuvered as a united front. This functioning as a unit was at that time, something revolutionary, and increased the strength of the Macedonian numbers many times over.

After the Companions came the archers. These covered the flanks of the troop formations. The artillery machines, also invented by Philip, were contraptions that threw stones. Alexander used these machines with great tactical success in battle. Then came the infamous phalanx which has already been described. These were rows of infantry, armed with thirteen foot long spears, which advanced as a tight wall, its members marching shield to shield and side by side, virtually locked against one another. The phalanx would advance, row by row, causing a terrifying effect. The phalanx was capable of forming itself into a mighty wedge, and functioned as a huge human tank. Time and time again, it proved an unshakable and unstoppable power. The phalanx was perhaps the most important element allowing Alexander to overcome armies much larger in number than his own. Alexander had an agile and creative approach to commanding his forces, and knew how to use their assets to his best advantage. His army was organized, mobile, and motivated. Alexander had the ability to choose the best force to use against the enemy's weakest point, at just the right moment. Often when the phalanx came into view, the opposing army would flee in terror.

Alexander's most promising general, Parmenion, was sent ahead to study the route the armies would take across the Hellespont (today called the Dardanelle straits) and into Asia. Meanwhile, Alexander bowed before statues of the god Zeus with thanksgiving for the successes had amassed so far, and prayer for the continued success of his campaigns.

Antipater, Alexander's trusted elderly general, was charged with the administration and leadership of Macedonia at home while the King was abroad. Antipater was provided a force of twelve thousand troops who stayed at home to back him up in case he needed to keep the peace in Greece or Macedonia. Alexander had explicit trust in Antipater and never worried about his own abandonment of the home front. As a younger man, Antipater had served under Philip, had always been extremely loyal to Alexander as a prince, and had taken a personal interest in his education. He remained loyal to Alexander, and when Philip died, Antipater is said to have rushed to the young man's side in order to be the first person to address Alexander as King.

While preparing the elder man for his task, Alexander made it clear that he was himself still King and had final say in all of Macedonia's affairs, his meaning being clear to Antipater that Olympias was to be thought of as Queen in name only, and would have no say in the administration of the Kingdom. Alexander trusted that Olympias could be held at bay by Antipater, and he was justified in so placing his confidence.

In the late spring of 334 B.C., as soon as the scouts and General Parmenion returned with advance intelligence concerning the crossing of the Dardanelles, Alexander made his final preparations for the beginning of the great adventure. The Macedonian naval fleet was inspected and food which would last the troops a month was boarded. Alexander recruited an elite group of non-military citizens to come along on the adventure. He chose the best scientists, such as botanists, geologists and geographers, as well as philosophers, authors, architects and secretaries to accompany the forces. He appointed historians to keep records of all the events as they unfolded.

Antigonus, Ptolemy, and Seleucus, his able and trusted generals, reported that the troops and the boats were ready. Sixty boats loaded with food enough to sustain the troops for a month sailed from the western end of the straits with their bows set for Asia. Alexander would never again set eyes on Pella. The remainder of his short life would be spent covering almost the entire known world on foot, in war, and glorious conquests.

Alexander Crosses to Asia

The crossing of the straits was uneventful and unopposed. It was smooth sailing and the weather favored them. Alexander rode on the bow of the flagship, decked out in his shining armor and elaborate head gear. The Persians could have caused some trouble here, since their naval fleet was far larger then Alexander's, but not a single enemy ship came on the horizon, and the Macedonians came ashore at Abydos without a hitch. As they arrived, Alexander paused on the bow of his ship and taking a running leap across the deck, threw his lightening shaped spear with all his strength at the coast of Asia. It flew, making a wide arch, until it dramatically came to rest stuck deep into the soil of Asia. Alexander disembarked to retrieve it, raised it on high, and declared that all of Asia would be his. Asia would be won by the spear!

Alexander's first activity on the soil of Asia was a visit to Illium, which had been ancient Troy. In fact, Troy had never been far from his mind, and he had dreamed of this visit for as long as he could remember. Ever since he had first read Homer's words as a boy, the heroes of the Trojan War had been close to his heart, and he longed to see the site of the first great Greek victory over Asia a thousand years before. While making his way down the rocky coast of Asia Minor to Troy, Alexander no doubt remembered the words of the Iliad which retold the brilliant Trojan horse trick, and thought of his beloved personal hero, Achilles.

When he reached Troy, the King made a sacrifice to the goddess Athena. In the temple, he came upon old preserved accoutrements, weapons and armor which were said to have belonged to Achilles. Alexander claimed the items as his by virtue of family inheritance and had them removed from the temple and readied for his use.

He had warned nobody of his visit so there was no royal welcome at first, but when word spread of the King's presence, the inhabitants welcomed him warmly as a descendent of the god Achilles, and led him to the grave of Achilles. Alexander's assembled troops followed him to the tomb, and along with his companion Hephaestion, he poured sacred oil over it, disrobed, and danced naked around it (all Greek customs of the time) before standing and making an impassioned speech. By the time they left Troy, all of Alexander's men believed he was the descendent of immortal deities.

Returning to his base near the Hellespont, Alexander took stock of his situation and made ready for the next advance. He had known before leaving Pella that his financial situation was quite desperate, and that the spoils of war, as well as crops they encountered on their journeys would have to sustain the armies in the long run. But even now, so near the beginning of the adventure, the coffers were seriously lacking – he counted a mere seventy talents. The King wished to distribute gifts to his companions anyway, so he offered them plots of his royal property in Pella. One of his captains asked concernedly what the King meant to keep for himself, and Alexander replied, "Hope!"

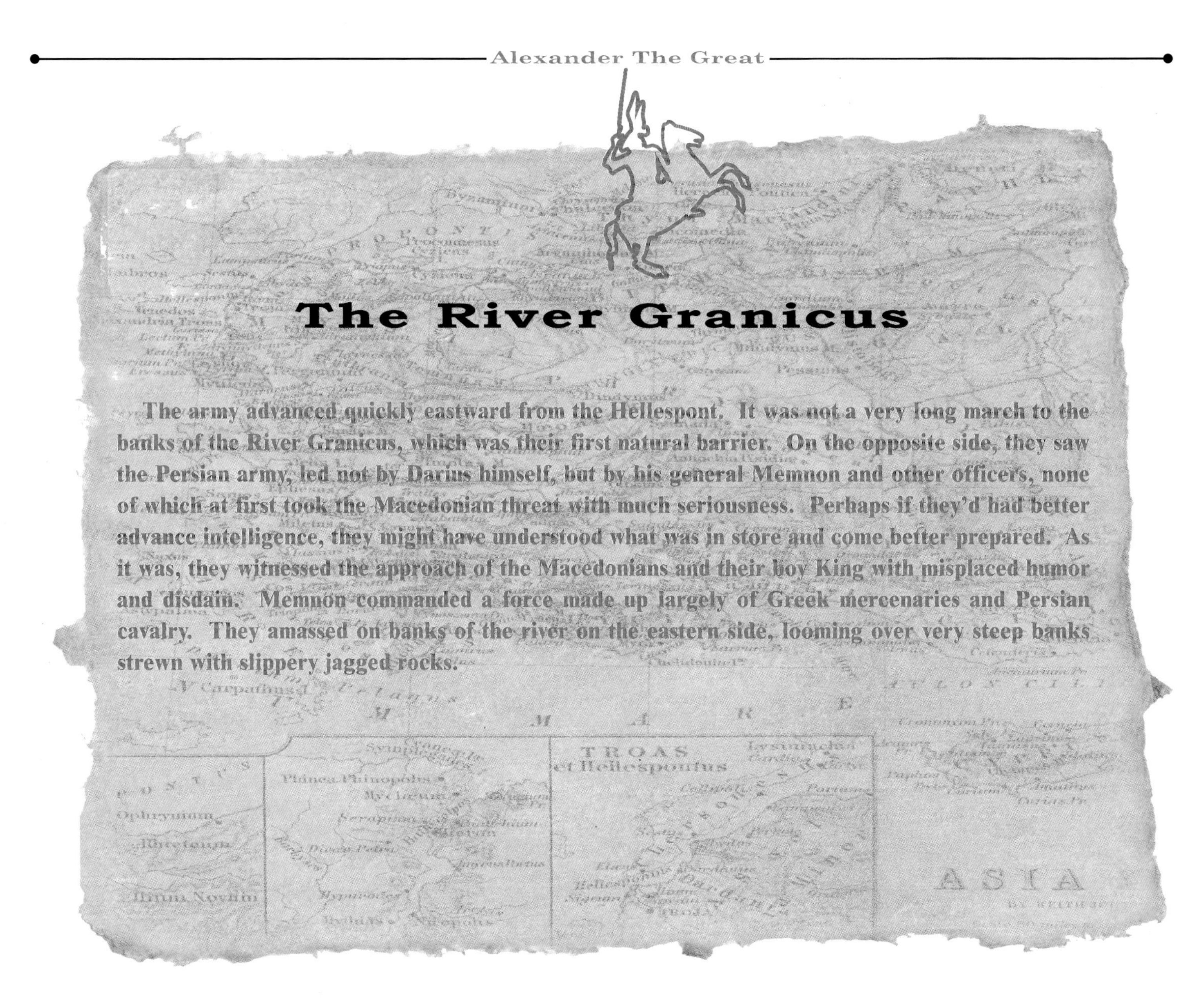

The River Granicus

The army advanced quickly eastward from the Hellespont. It was not a very long march to the banks of the River Granicus, which was their first natural barrier. On the opposite side, they saw the Persian army, led not by Darius himself, but by his general Memnon and other officers, none of which at first took the Macedonian threat with much seriousness. Perhaps if they'd had better advance intelligence, they might have understood what was in store and come better prepared. As it was, they witnessed the approach of the Macedonians and their boy King with misplaced humor and disdain. Memnon commanded a force made up largely of Greek mercenaries and Persian cavalry. They amassed on banks of the river on the eastern side, looming over very steep banks strewn with slippery jagged rocks.

The hot June afternoon sun beat down on the troops, and one of Alexander's officers reminded him that June was traditionally an unlucky month to do battle. Alexander considered this briefly before he calmly answered, "We'll turn back the calendar. For us it is still May". Parmenion approached Alexander worriedly and advised him that the crossing of the Granicus should wait until the next morning as evening would soon fall. In fact, Parmenion and the other generals were a bit panicked at the sight of the river and the conditions under which they would have to fight the Persian force waiting for them on the opposite bank. They knew that because of the current of the river, the crossing would have to be done in a straight column, making them vulnerable to the Persians. Parmenion told Alexander that he feared the river was a dangerous trap for them. This comment too was brushed aside by the King who responded "The Hellespont would blush with shame if it knew that after we braved its crossing we became afraid to cross a mere river!"

Many have characterized Alexander's decision as reckless and foolhardy, however it must be remembered that Alexander was not an irresponsible leader. He deeply cared for his soldiers and would not expose them to danger on a whim. Rather, he held a deep and abiding belief in his mission invincibility and his ability to lead them to victory, despite outward appearances and conditions. He set an example for his men by his own tremendous courage and conviction.

Alexander jumped astride Bucephalus, and called for the crossing to commence. He and his steed plunged into the water amid flying Persian arrows as the struggle began. The Persians had no trouble recognizing the Macedonian King, since besides riding his massive horse, his shield had royal markings and his helmet sported an enormous white plume.

As the Macedonians clamored across the river, they were met by the enemy with swords drawn, and the two sides fought at such close range they could see the sweat glistening on their opponents' faces. . During the fight, Alexander's spear was severed in half. Though Alexander bravely fought on with half a weapon, his groom called out to one of the bodyguards who relinquished his own spear to the King. One of Darius' top commanders, his son-in-law Mithridates, engaged the Macedonian King and his captains in hand to hand combat. Alexander was wounded, first in the thigh when a dart hit him, and then by Mithridate's javelin which was aimed with precision and considerable force at the King. Mithridate hoisted himself up to a standing position in his stirrups, and with a mighty roar he pounded his javelin toward the King from above. The battle-ax came crashing down onto

Alexander's head, shaving the crest off his helmet and destroying the white plume. Bucephalus lost his footing as a result of the blow, and Alexander was thrown off the steed. Lying vulnerable on the ground, he was surely only seconds away from being killed by a Persian noble who rode up to him brandishing his sword. At that moment, however, Cleitus rushed in and rammed his spear through the Persian's body. Cleitus ("Black") had saved Alexander's life.

While the King and the Persian high officers were engaged in one on one sword combat, the rest of the Macedonians had managed to get across the river. As their numbers grew on the eastern bank, they quickly formed into their phalanx. The sight of this demonstration of Macedonian discipline and organization caused the Persians to begin to lose their nerve and most of them fled. Alexander managed to remount Bucephalus as his men raised a mighty cheer.

The Macedonian victory was complete, and by all accounts Alexander's men had suffered very few casualties. The maximum loss recorded is about one hundred men. As would be often the case, in the aftermath of the first great Asian victory Alexander exhibited great fluctuations and extremes of character. His treatment of the victims and the heroes of warfare illustrates this vividly.

Most of the fallen had been in the companion cavalry, which made the first assault. Alexander ordered statues made of these men on the shores of the river, and all of the dead were buried on the day after the battle. The burial was respectful and solemn, each soldier being interred with his armor and weapon. In addition, the families of the fallen were notified and granted freedom from taxation for the rest of their lives. The wounded men enjoyed Alexander's compassionate attention. He paid a visit to each and every one of them, called them heroes, and listened patiently and compassionately as they told their stories and showed him their injuries. Alexander's own wounds were carefully dressed and bandaged by his best and most trusted physician, Philip.

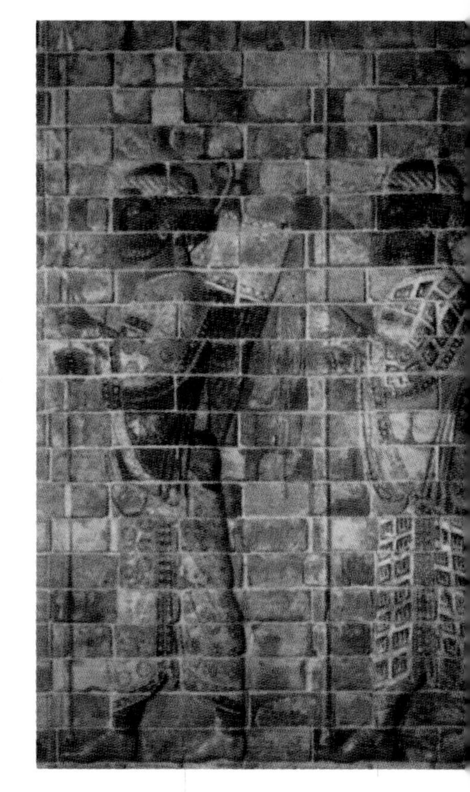

The enemy dead received dignified burials as well, be they Persian or Greek mercenaries. Alexander believed that to fight and die in battle was worthy of being called heroism – even if one died for the "wrong" side. Those Greeks that were captured, however, suffered perhaps an even worse fate than death, as Alexander made sure they were sent back to Macedonia in chains to be sold as slaves, as punishment for joining a foreign army in fighting their own people.

The battle of Granicus had been a tremendous gamble, which turned into an astounding victory. Alexander's confidence had never wavered. His great courage, his enormous good fortune, and the loyalty of his men, especially the "Black" had carried the day. The Greek historian Callisthenes, a nephew of Aristotle, described the battle of Granicus as the work of the Goddess Nemesis, who used Alexander to avenge the Persian attacks on Greece a century before.

Asia Minor Hails Alexander

Alexander and his men took a breather after the battle of Granicus. They did not chase the retreating Persians, and any natives who appeared before them in surrender were allowed to return peacefully to their homes.

Leaving Darius to his own devices for the time being, Alexander decided to march his army down Asia Minor, making sure it was secure and grabbing up communities all along the coast. He marched southward into Halicarnassus, which surrendered to him after a few days of siege. Ephesus surrendered without a fight, and there Alexander established a base from which he proceeded to Miletus, Lysippus, Pisidians, Sardis, and other cities, taKing them too, with little or no combat. Word of the young King's abilities and his frightful armies had preceded him, and few were willing to draw him into conflict. One by one they liberated the Greek cities of Asia.

Alexander had divided his forces for the securing of Asia Minor. Parmenion took half of the army to the Persian controlled hill areas and Phrygia, while Alexander led troops to the Greed cities on the coast. Very little looting was allowed by the Macedonian-Greek forces and Alexander liberated the cities compassionately, allowing them to continue to run their own affairs in a semi-democratic manner. In Melitus, the inner city was held by a group of Greek mercenaries, and Alexander could easily have taught them the same lesson he had taught the rebels in Thebes, but rather than simply overpower them, he chose to negotiate, offering the mercenaries pardons, and even, our of respect for the great courage of the mercenaries, posts in his own army - if they would surrender the city. Melitus thus fell quite easily into Alexander's hands. The Macedonians took control of the high country of what is now central Turkey and snapped up possession of several key ports on the southern coast, including Caria, Lycia and Pamphylia.

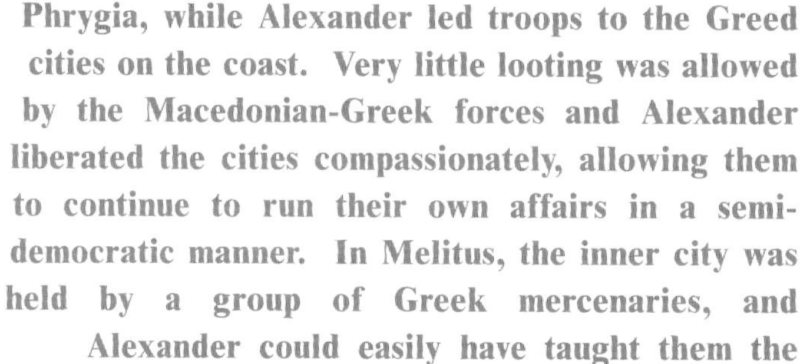

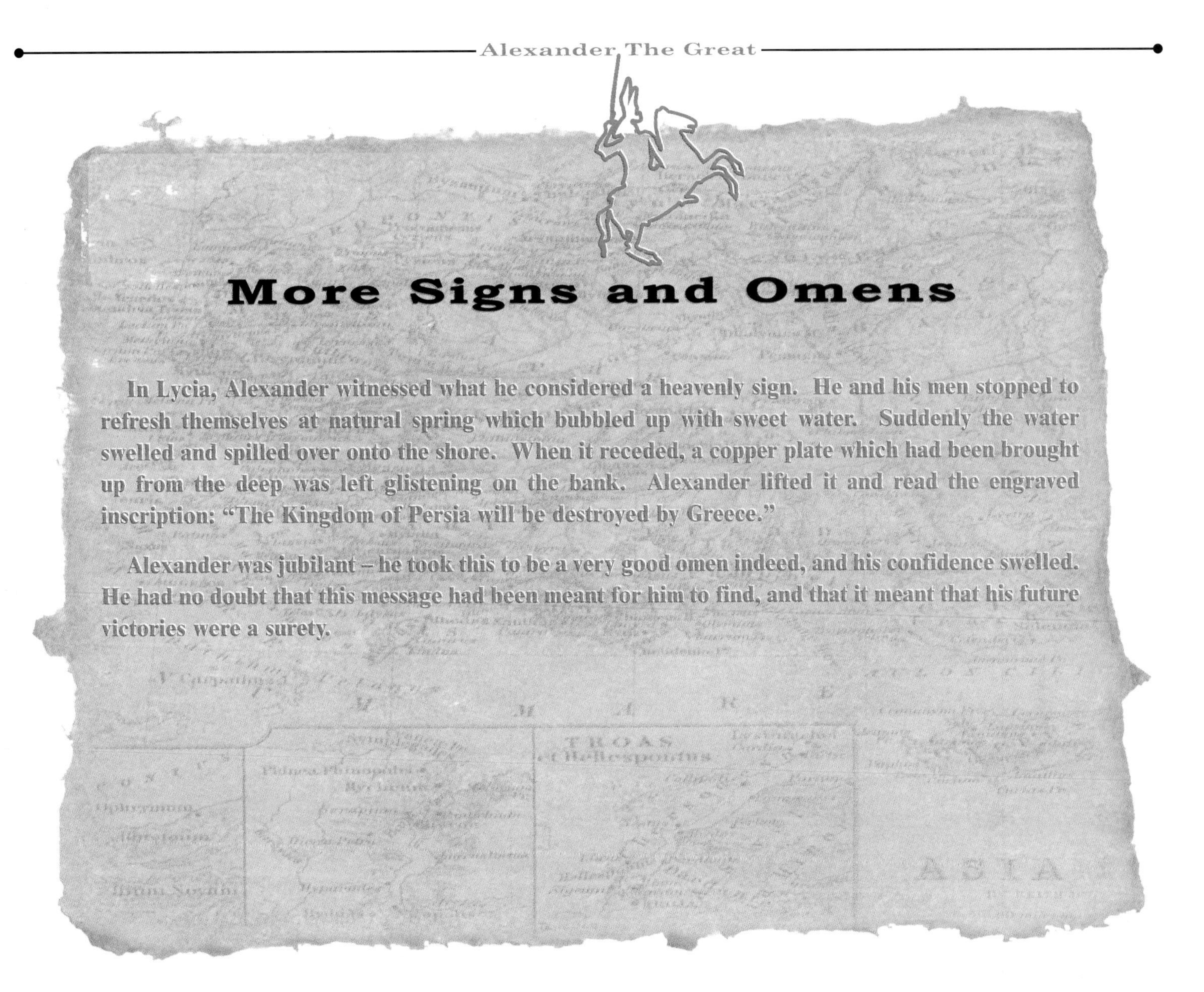

More Signs and Omens

In Lycia, Alexander witnessed what he considered a heavenly sign. He and his men stopped to refresh themselves at natural spring which bubbled up with sweet water. Suddenly the water swelled and spilled over onto the shore. When it receded, a copper plate which had been brought up from the deep was left glistening on the bank. Alexander lifted it and read the engraved inscription: “The Kingdom of Persia will be destroyed by Greece.”

Alexander was jubilant – he took this to be a very good omen indeed, and his confidence swelled. He had no doubt that this message had been meant for him to find, and that it meant that his future victories were a surety.

In the spring of 333 B.C. Alexander had marched his troops southward until they reached the Phrygian capital of Gordium, which was situated near what is today Ankara, Turkey. Gordium, according to Greek mythology, had been the seat of the Kingdom of Midas in the eighth century B.C. Midas was famous for his tremendous wealth and unlimited ability to attract more (what we call in today's vernacular the "Midas touch"). When Alexander and his men arrived, they were led to a well-guarded building which housed a very old chariot. The chariot was preserved as a supposed relic from the time of Midas, and it was secured by a rope which tied its shaft to its axle with an extremely complicated and complex knot. This knot had become notorious and people had come from all over the world to try their hand at untying it, for legend had it that he who would succeed at loosening the knot would become the King of Asia.

Alexander was led into the chamber of the chariot, and taking one look at the famous Gordian knot; he drew his sword, and sliced the knot apart with a single swift stroke. The onlookers were shocked and amazed. Apparently it had never occurred to anyone to use this method of "untying" the knot! Alexander simply took this as more evidence of his invincibility and the inevitability of his conquering of Asia. That night there was a fierce thunderstorm, which the King was grateful for as further

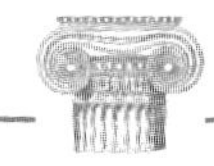

Alexander's Sexuality

No modern biography of Alexander would be complete without at least a mention of sexual behavior. This is because of the present-day preoccupation with such subjects rather than because the subject is particularly fascinating where our young king was concerned. For all intents and purposes, Alexander conducted his sex life, such as it was, along very respectable lines for a 4th Century B.C. Macedonian. Any attempt to pigeonhole him or his behavior according to 21st century norms would be worse than ridiculous. For example, many have asked "was Alexander homosexual?" One must heave a sigh before answering, and preface the response with a hefty dose of understanding of the sexual mores of his time. There simply was no label

proof that the heavens and deities had proclaimed him King of Asia. To this day, the expression "cut the Gordian knot" means to do the impossible, or to solve a seemingly unsolvable problem.

While still in Gordium, only weeks before his next serious encounter with Darius' armies, Alexander experienced a critical illness which may have been a form of malaria. He had a raging fever which none of his physicians were able to relieve. Day after day he lay in a feverish stupor, and many began to despair that this would be the end for the 22 year old King! Alexander managed to rouse himself to a sitting position and ask for his most trusted medical man, Philip the Arcanian to be brought to him. Philip arrived and told the King that treatment was at hand – he would cure him. Philip prepared a potion and returned to the King's tent to administer the medication. At the moment that he handed Alexander a flask and instructed him to swallow its contents, a messenger arrived on the double, and breathlessly handed a note to the King. The memo was from Parmenion. The general had been given the information from his intelligence unit that Philip the physician was actually an assassin hired by Darius to do away with Alexander. "Beware Philip", said the note. Logic would have Alexander immediately become suspect of the proffered liquid, fearing poisoning. Parmenion, after all, was a proven friend and would not have delivered information ill-gotten or incredible. But the King had already formed his impression of Philip, based not on intelligence but on his own observations and feelings.

which corresponds with our modern moniker "homosexual". Most people, especially men, were what we would today term "bi-sexual". There was absolutely no stigma whatever on sexual activity with a same sex partner, those who engaged in it would not have thought of themselves as having an unusual or minority sexual orientation. The taboo against same sex relationships only began to evolve hundreds of years after Alexander's death.

It is generally accepted fact that a catalog of Alexander's lovers would include a larger portion of males than females. This may have been a matter of convenience rather than conscious choice. His closest relationship of any kind, save perhaps his relationship with his mother, was to his friend Hephaestion. There can be little doubt that the two engaged in sex with one another throughout their lives. Hephaestion was probably Alexander's first lover, as well as his first love, and perhaps even his deepest love. While as a rule, boys were initiated into sex by an adult male, in Alexander's case the boys seem to have coupled with one another while still quite young.

Alexander did not hesitate. He read the note, and grasping it in one hand, he accepted the cup of medicine from Philip with the other, and quickly gulped it down. As he drank, he handed Philip the note, and watched as the physician read its contents. Philip was amazed that the King had dared take his potion after receiving such a warning. Philip

Save for Hephaestion, Alexander's youth seemed strangely almost asexual. He certainly is not known for being a great lover, and most historians portray him as having little interest in sex beyond what was necessary to consummate his marriages. There was no female love interest in Alexander's life until well into his expedition, which leads some to postulate that his main orientation was homosexuality. We have several comments from historians concerning Alexander's polite and correct behavior with captive women in his entourage, most notably the female family members of the Persian King Darius. At no time did Alexander behave with impropriety toward the woman as perhaps another leader of the time might have, and this is seen by some as more evidence that his preference was for men.

The fact that he married at least two woman and was born two sons (both died in childhood) points out the fact the he was functionally what we would today term bi-sexual. Whether he preferred male over female partners is open to conjecture. No one has quoted Alexander making any sort of declaration on the matter, and sex was not a priority in his life or identity. His marriages are not

was indeed an innocent man, and loyal to the King, but how could Alexander have been so sure? Sure enough to risk his life! Alexander's symptoms worsened briefly, but after that he quickly recovered his former vigor and strength. His intuition and confidence in his own inherent judgment of character had saved his life, for he would surely have perished without Philip's treatment. Alexander took this episode as another message from the gods that he was indeed invincible, if only he would follow his own inner guidance and knowledge!

chronicled as having been love stories of huge import, but Alexander's preoccupation was with other things. History suffers no shortage of mighty leaders who also fancied themselves "God's gift" to the opposite sex, and who waxed eloquent, verbally and behaviorally in the areas of sex and love. Alexander's thoughts and ambitions lay elsewhere. He would no doubt shake his head in wonder that we discuss this matter at all.

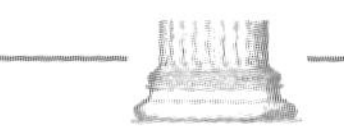

The Battle of Issus

It was to be almost a full year after the battle of Granicus before Alexander's army would again clash with the hosts of King Darius. The western coast of Asia Minor was firmly under Alexander by the early months of 333 B.C. when Parmenion reunited his division with Alexander's at Gordium. Together they made ready to continue southward toward the Mediterranean. Alexander's long range plan was to take the northern coast of the sea, and then to continue down its eastern coast.

During the respite of Alexander's illness, the Persian navy had sailed from its ports in the Mediterranean to the Aegean Sea. A huge fleet of three hundred warships manned by sixty thousand troops had anchored at the various Aegean islands, causing a threat to communication lines between Alexander's army and Macedonia and Greece. Alexander sent an urgent message home to Antipater requesting more troops and reinforcement of his defensive lines on Greek mainland.

In late spring of 333 B.C. Alexander's armies were poised to march through the mountains to the "Gates of Cilicia", the region which formed a passageway to Syria and the center of the Persian Empire (what is today Iran), through a steep range of mountains. The army marched through the summer, while Darius and his much larger force simultaneously trekked northward, sticking to the flat terrain on the eastern side of the mountain. Alexander overtook them, staying close to the coast. The inevitable meeting of the two armies at Issus was to be a very decisive battle indeed.

Darius and his men tried to lure Alexander into combat in the eastern valley, where the open plains would be a far better environment for his massive battalions and put Alexander's smaller force at the disadvantage. Alexander waited to see whether Darius would move first. When time passed and Darius became impatient he asked his advisors for council. Amyntas, a defector from Alexander's army who knew the Macedonian force first hand, advised Darius unequivocally to hold his ground in the plains where his huge army machine would be able to maneuver and not to allow himself to venture into the narrow passes where even with his tremendous numbers he would be an easy mark for Alexander. He insisted that if Darius would only be patient, Alexander would eventually venture into the plains with his armies, and that this was the Persians' only chance for victory. Others, however, advised Darius to get on the move, saying that Alexander delayed out of fear of the Persians. They flattered the King with lavish descriptions of the way the Persian force was about to smash an enemy that was losing its nerve. Darius chose to believe the majority of the advisors rather than Amyntas' wise advice, and proceeded to commit a fatal tactical error. He ordered his generals to attempt to severe Alexander's communications from behind, encircling the Macedonian and Greek armies from the rear and cutting him them off from the sea. In so doing, Darius' men trapped themselves in the narrow break in the mountains, where they were forced to meet the Alexander at Issus.

Alexander, when he received word that the Persians were actually behind him, had a hard time believing this illogical turn of events at first, and sent boats on a scouting mission to see if it was fact. When his informants returned with the report that yes, Darius' force was amassed in the rear, he called a meeting of all his officers, and sitting astride Bucephalus, he addressed them passionately. He reminded the men of their previous glorious victories, praising them for their tremendous ability to look danger in the face unflinchingly. Pointing out that Darius had for some reason moved himself and his armies into a foolish predicament, he was certain that even if this had not occurred, victory would have been Alexander's, since in any case the Persians were a cowardly lot that for centuries had become used to a soft life of luxuries, while he and his men were used to the Spartan austerity which made men tough and brave. The Persians and the Greek mercenaries who fought on their side did so for pay, while the Macedonian and Greek soldiers of Alexander fought for their cause, and for revenge, so that their hearts would be in it ever the more. He told them that he believed it had been God himself who moved the Persians into a position favorable to him and his men, proving that it was their manifest destiny to overtake the whole of Asia. Alexander's speech praised his men and expressed his gratitude and pride in their courage and skill. Lastly, he stressed, "The Persians fight under Darius, while you have Alexander!" By the time he had finished enumerating the advantages they had over the Persians, not an officer in his army suffered from low morale or lack of confidence over what was to take place.

Alexander knew he was far outnumbered - approximately one hundred thousand to thirty thousand - and it would take cunning, speed, and precision to defeat the Persians. He ordered Parmenio to lead the left flank – a force of Greek soldiers who were in for quite a difficult fight. Meanwhile Alexander lost no time beginning the march of his right wing formation toward the Persian camp, forming his men into a mighty wedge which drove deep into enemy lines, dispersing them and causing confusion in their ranks. Darius tried to reorganize his troops and slow the Macedonian charge, but his superior numbers were of no use in this state of disarray. Alexander took advantage of their situation and ordered another crushing attack from his left wing force. At some point, Alexander was wounded badly in the thigh, and losing his balance because of the wound, almost received a fatal slash from a Persian sword. At the critical second, one of the royal bodyguards sliced the arm off the offending Persian, and Alexander once again gave death the slip. He rallied his strength and the battle took a decisive turn when Alexander himself led the infantry phalanx roaring toward the center of Persian camp, aiming directly for Darius himself. At the sight and sound of the phalanx the Persians lost their nerve and panic ensued in their ranks. They were overrun by Alexander's men and many tens of thousands of them perished while thousands more fled eastward for their lives. King Darius led the fleeing pack in his gilded chariot, driving his chariot as fast as his horses would go over the flatlands. When he came to hilly terrain he jumped from his chariot and stripping himself of his heavy armor and mantle, and leaving his weapons as well, he jumped on a horse and continued his frenzied flight. Darius had abandoned his immediate family as well as his entire court harem, not to speak of his considerable treasure.

When the battle died down and Darius was gone, Alexander did not pursue him very far. As soon as night fell, he returned to camp in order to see to the aftermath of battle. As was his custom, he respectfully buried the dead or cremated them on decorated pyres and dispatched the ashes back to Greece and Macedonia. Surgeons tended to the wounded, and each one received a royal visit and commendation. Some of his exhausted veterans were sent home to visit family, amid praise and appreciation from their commander. Soldiers who had committed heroic acts in battle were addressed by name as the King inspected the troops. He remembered them and cared for them as brothers, and his affection and pride in his men was genuine. Morale remained extremely high in Alexander's army.

While the spoils of war had been grabbed by the victorious soldiers, the court of Darius had been captured, but remained untouched. It was recognized that this now belonged to Alexander alone. Alexander rode up to Darius' royal tent camp and inspected its contents. Darius had abandoned glorious riches of all kinds, in quantities which defied imagination. There were chests full of gold and precious gems and jewels of all description, as well as rare silk fabrics and luxurious perfumes. Alexander had never seen such a grand collection, as the Macedonian and Greek courts were never so opulent or luxurious, and his own lifestyle was quite Spartan. He was awed by what he saw, and declared that Darius' private domain was "majestic indeed ". He saw for the first time what it could mean to be King. Alexander's boyishness took over for a time, and he allowed himself to revel in his newfound bounty, and to bask in royal ease. He ordered Darius' servants to draw him a bath in Darius' ornate tub, laughing with glee over the realization that is was now Alexander's own tub!

From among Darius' affects, Alexander chose gifts to send back to Olympias, who enjoyed receiving part of

the booty after every battle. For himself, he claimed a small chest studded with precious gems. He placed in it his dog-eared copy of the Iliad which he had carried with him throughout his adventure. It was the same book which Aristotle had given him as a gift many years earlier. He now had a fitting container for this treasured volume.

Once Alexander had made himself presentable and rested to regain his strength after the battle, he turned his attention to the abandoned and forlorn family of Darius. The beautiful young Statira, Darius' wife (she was also his sister) and her infant son sat with the King's mother, Sisygambis, and two of his daughters, princesses of Persia, in the royal tent, waiting and wondering fearfully what their fate was to be. They needn't have been frightened however, as Alexander treated them with all of the chivalry and respect due to true royals. Although technically the family members were prisoners of war, Alexander stole nothing of their personal affects, allowing no looting of their belongings and letting them keep their jewelry, garments, and other objects. When the women were brought before him, he and Hephaestion received them sitting on identical throne-like chairs and decked out in outfits that resembled one another. The women were immensely distraught and weeping. Darius' mother mistook the taller Hephaestion for the King and fell to the ground in front of him begging for mercy. Alexander was amused, but not offended, and he assured the woman that it was of no matter whatever, since "Hephaestion too, is "an Alexander". This remark illustrates both Alexander's profound respect and confidence in his friend, and his lack of needless conceit.

It was explained to Alexander that the women were crying out of grief at Darius supposed death. His chariot and other discarded items had been returned to the camp, and the natural assumption had been made that he'd been killed. Alexander assured them that Darius had escaped and was very much alive, and furthermore, that he, Alexander meant them absolutely no harm. Aristotle had impressed Alexander early on with his teachings concerning proper behavior with women, and the young King had very much taken these mores to heart. The King was still in regular contact with the great teacher, and reported his exploits and accomplishments in frequent letters. That the esteemed philosopher should still be proud of his student remained a source of motivation for the young man. Alexander looked right at the pretty queen and declared "I do not fight against Darius, I fight for his Kingdom". At a later date, when Alexander released Stateira and she had an opportunity to return to the Persians, she refused to leave!

King of Asia

Having been wounded in the thigh quite severely, Alexander required a period of rest and recuperation after the Battle of Issus. The twenty-three year old King had already accomplished an amazing amount since the beginning of the Asian adventure. He had much to contemplate and still more to plan and look forward to. Alexander was not one for idleness, however, and in fact when it was forced upon him he reacted badly, falling into self-destructive habits such as heavy drinking of alcohol. His need for constant stimulation, when not being assuaged by the activities of a conquering hero, found secondary satisfaction in drunkenness.

During the respite after the battle of Issus, Alexander received an envoy that had been sent from Darius. The Persian King had meanwhile rejoined many of his surviving troops, and marched quickly toward the Euphrates River, and eventually Cyprus, and Egypt. The envoy requested the release of Darius' family, and in addition, he handed Alexander a letter which contained an offer of friendship and a proposed peace agreement. Alexander could hardly give the matter any gravity, since he had set out on this adventure with every intention of ruling the empire in its entirety! He informed Darius that he had invaded Persia to avenge the crime of Darius' ancestors who unprovoked, attacked Greece so many years ago. He further reiterated to Darius a full syllabus of crimes committed by the Persian Empire against the Greek and Macedonian people in general and his father, Philip, among others, in particular. He reminded Darius that the two Kings were not equals – that indeed anything Darius had once possessed was now Alexander's. Darius was admonished to send no further letters or messengers, and that if he wished to communicate with Alexander he should brave his countenance in person. Most importantly, Alexander made it clear that would stop at nothing but full surrender of all his adversaries, including Darius, and universal recognition of himself as King of Asia.

The Siege of Tyre

It was with relief and excitement that Alexander finally declared himself and his regimens ready to move on – to continue the march southward from Syria, along the coast of the Mediterranean, into Phoenicia, what is today Lebanon and Israel, and Egypt. The plan was to take the many Persian seaports along this coast, giving him full control of the Mediterranean and Aegean Seas. As he advanced southward, the first few ports fell with little effort. Aradus, Byblos and Sidon surrendered quickly to the advancing Macedonians, welcoming Alexander as a conquering hero and giving him full honors.

In January of 332 B.C., Alexander and his men reached the city of Tyre, a large Persian naval base and residence of many of the crewmen. The navy men were known to be fierce, even fanatical fighters and considered enemies by all their neighboring city-states. The city of Tyre was situated on an island which was far enough off the coast that the water around it was five meters deep. The city was a veritable fortress, with colossal one hundred and fifty foot walls and two well-protected harbors. The massive walls which surrounded the city came virtually to the water's edge, making the city all but impenetrable.

Alexander could not continue on without taking Tyre, as difficult as this might prove. It was vital for him to control the eastern Mediterranean to assure safe passage of supplies and communications at all times. He who ruled the sea would ultimately prevail, he was certain. Since landing on the island and taking the city by force was in essence, impossible, the Macedonians tried to bombard the citadel walls from the sea. Alexander sent his ships to close range, equipped with gigantic catapults and towers which brought his men right up to the tops of the city walls, but the ships were sunk, one after the other, by the citizens of Tyre who dropped huge boulders onto their decks. There was no other choice but to close off access to Tyre from the sea and lay siege to the island. Cutting the city off from supply was his only hope at wearing it down as long as its inhabitants refused to surrender. Unfortunately for Alexander, Tyre had its own wells of fresh water and had already stocked up on supplies enough for quite an extended period of time.

During the siege, the Macedonian and Greek engineers went to work on a land bridge which would connect Tyre with the shore. This project entailed several months of intense physical labor for hundreds of men, piling timber and stones onto a two hundred foot wide strip of sea. The work was dangerous, since the builders were under constant attack from the fort city, and there were many setbacks, but at last the causeway was complete and solid firmament connected Tyre to the mainland. The effect was a permanent change in the geography of the place. Tyre was no longer an island.

When the causeway was ready, Alexander used it as a land base from which to attack the already besieged citizens of Tyre. Alexander's giant siege machines battered the walls of the city. Even now, however, they fiercely resisted, and pushed back the Macedonians time after time, using giant catapults and boulders. The final battle for Tyre actually came when out of one of Tyre's harbors a warship roared into action, threatening the Macedonians on the causeway. Alexander called for reinforcements and ships from Rhodes, Sidon and Cyprus and these arrived in short order. A fierce naval battle raged, and at long last Tyre was forced to surrender. The siege of Tyre had lasted over seven months.

While he'd still been involved in the events of Tyre, Alexander had received another message from Darius. The Persian King this time offered a large sum of money for the ransom of his mother, wife, and children. Furthermore, he proposed to recognize the sovereignty of Alexander over all territories between the Euphrates River and the Aegean Sea. The rest of the empire would remain under King Darius, and the two would seal their agreement by becoming family by virtue of the marriage of Alexander to Darius' daughter. Parmenio, upon hearing the terms of the proposed agreement, heartily urged the King to sign it. He said it would put Alexander in a favorable position and that then the adventure could come to an honorable end. If he were King, declared Parmenio, he would send Darius an answer in the affirmative.

Alexander's respectful retort to his second in command was that indeed he too would agree to Darius' plan - if he were Parmenio! Since he was Alexander, however, his response was quite different. Nothing had changed since their last correspondence to dampen Alexander's vision or his belief that he was the rightful King of Asia. Darius had no choice but to come to terms with the fact that Alexander would not be bribed nor bought, and that there was more confrontation to come.

Dessert Sands

After Tyre, in late 332 B.C. Alexander and his army enjoyed a happy march southward along the Phoenician coast of what is now modern Israel. The towns they passed all hailed Alexander and his thousands of proud troops, and accepted his control gladly. He bypassed the mountainous inland city of Jerusalem, the capital of Judea, believing it to be an unimportant hideaway for priests and of no strategic importance for his mission. Besides, he respected the priestly rule of the holy temple there. Hugging the coast, Alexander's armies made there way down the eastern shores of the Mediterranean, while their vessels sailed in parallel with supplies and food on board. The climate became more arid as they wended their way southward. Their march proceeded unimpeded until they reached the city of Gaza, the last garrison of civilization before the vast dessert which separated Phoenicia from Egypt. The city, standing several miles from the seacoast, was built like a brick fortress, and stood on a partially man-made hill of clay surrounded by loose sand. The Arab inhabitants led by the stubborn and proud Batis had no intention whatever of welcoming the invaders, and made it clear that they believed their city sealed and impregnable against the handsome young King of Macedonia. Batis was a staunch supporter of Darius, and would remain loyal to him at all costs.

The Gazans were up against a will even greater than their however, and Gaza had to be taken before the Macedonians could continue their mission to Egypt. Alexander consulted his engineers as to the best way to proceed against Gaza, and was perhaps momentarily nonplussed to hear that they were a bit frightened by the unusual way the city was built and fortified. Gaza would definitely be a challenge, they reported. As they contemplated the form the first attack would take, Alexander suddenly noticed a crow overhead that seemed to be flying strangely, as if to attract his attention. The crow was carrying a pebble in its claws, and as it passed over Alexander it dropped it directly onto the King's unhelmeted head. The crow then flew out of range of sight, leaving Alexander with the feeling he had just been witness to another sign from the gods. He summoned Aristander, who never wandered far from his master, and asked for an interpretation. Alexander listened gravely as his seer explained that Gaza would indeed be taken, but not in one day, and that on this particular day Alexander was in danger of being wounded and must take careful personal precautions. Aristander even suggested postponing the attack on Gaza until conditions were more favorable for the King. Alexander listened, but ordered the campaign to begin immediately.

It was decided that the best course of action was to dig out the foundations of the fortress walls closing in the city. While this was being accomplished, they distracted the Gazans with frontal attacks at their city gates. Alexander tried to heed Aristander's warning and at first kept himself away from the front lines of attack. He was not used to standing by while his men fought however, and this fighting was particularly heavy and brutal. It seemed the Macedonian troops were tiring and in need of their commander to raise their spirits and show a good example. When he could no longer bear hiding in safety while others struggled, he leapt into the fray, forgetting the portended danger to his person. Sure enough, one of the missiles pouring forth from above the Gazan walls pierced Alexander's armor, wounding him in the shoulder. Alexander was delighted! The wound caused him considerable pain, but was not fatal and was quickly tended to by Philip and his other physicians If this part of the prophecy had panned out, he reasoned, then surely it all would come true, meaning that Gaza would indeed fall, although not today.

Alexander ordered artillery backup so that he would have an arsenal similar to that which he used against Tyre. This too, it seemed, could turn into a prolonged siege. When the heavy artillery arrived by sea, platforms were built enabling the guns to be set up at enough height to cause severe damage to the walls of Gaza city. Meanwhile, the digging below ground continued.

The siege of Gaza continued for a period of two months with Alexander's men working steadily to weaken the fortress. When at last enough damage to the wall had been done, ladders were brought by which Alexander's men clamored into the city. Their was brave and insistent fighting on the part of the Gazans, with each man fighting hand to hand with the conquerors until at last every Gazan defender lay dead and the city was taken. Only the women and children were left. Alexander ordered them rounded up and sold as slaves, leaving Gaza an empty ghost town. The town was repopulated by neighboring tribes whom Alexander settled there as a base for future operations.

Alexander Enters Egypt

By the time Alexander as ready to enter Egypt, in 331 B.C. he was accepted in the worldwide consciousness as the Greek commander. Macedonia and Greece had effectively merged, making them one whole, under the name of Greece. At a recent meeting of the city-states Alexander had been given an additional vote of confidence and renamed the Captain General of Greece. Only Sparta had voted against him.

After the Gazan victory, Alexander rallied his troops and they headed across the dessert to Egypt, again following the shoreline of the Mediterranean as it curved back toward the west as supply ships sailed close by. In a week's time they had crossed the great Sinai dessert and arrived at the gateway to Egypt – Pelusium, on the banks of the Nile River. There Alexander set up a garrison and sent his fleet along the Nile to Memphis to wait for him.

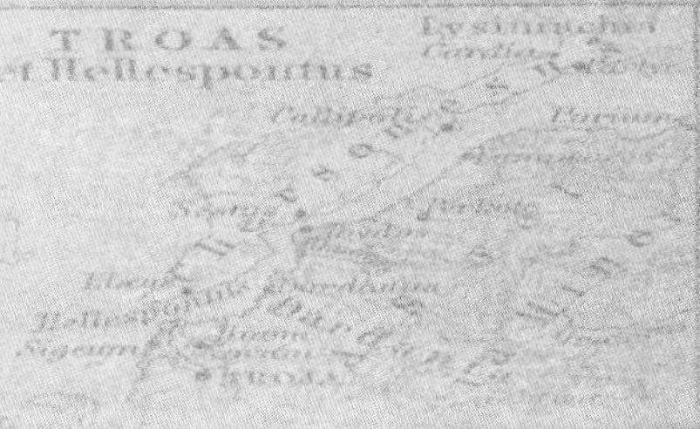

Egypt had for the past two hundred years been part of the Persian Empire. Their governor, Mazaces, had served unhappily under Darius, and the latter had not earned him more respect by fleeing the Greek forces at Issus. Persian rule had been a heavy yoke for the Egyptians, and there was no love lost between them and Darius who had forced them to adopt Persian customs and pray to the Persian gods. Mazaces had already heard all about Alexander's exploits in Phoenicia and he was aware that Syria too was already under Greek rule. He saw no reason to resist Alexander, and in fact welcomed him as a deliverer and liberator, and instructed his people to do the same. In truth, even had Mazaeus been inclined to resist, he had not much of an army at his command and he was geographically completely isolated from any Persian outpost that might have assisted him. Egypt hailed Alexander, Pharaoh of Egypt.

Alexander with the God Min

In this situation Alexander was a most benevolent and benign King. His nature was not cruel unless provoked, so where he was welcomed as he was in Egypt, he never found it necessary to perform acts of violence or force to prove himself. In fact, he saw to the restoration of liberties previously denied the Egyptian people by the Persians. Thebes, Tyre, and Gaza had known the full extent of his ability to be extremely vengeful and even heartless, because these cities had forced him to fight and to fight hard – to lose his own men, and to "waste" his time in battle when he could be moving forward carrying out what he considered his manifest destiny. When he did not have to fight, Alexander was never destructive; he was in fact constructive – promoting the local cultures and religions of each of the peoples he overtook. He promoted Greek culture as well, without limiting local freedoms. Egypt saw this right from the beginning with the establishment of the great city of Alexandria.

When Alexander arrived at the small trading port of Naukratis, he declared it the site of a city which would bear his name. This piece of land at the mouth of the Nile, overlooking the sea and with a small island slightly offshore seemed the perfect place for Alexander to establish what was to be the greatest of all the cities he founded in his name.

It would be a straight shot across the Mediterranean to Greece, and the position was ideal for trade with the entire area. Indeed, since Tyre was sacked, there was need for another port to take over the commercial activities that had been centered there. To the south, the city would be connected to the Red Sea by the Nile River and a canal, opening to the Indian Ocean. Alexander was right in his estimation that this spot was a point of power. He ordered planning of the great city to begin without delay. It was not just to be any city – it would be uniquely beautiful and its plan would be revolutionary – different from any Greek or Persian city before it.

The Greek architect Dinocrates was commissioned with the design of Alexandria. While basically he followed the traditional Greek plan, the flatness and openness of the terrain allowed for longer avenues, many squares, and straight intersections. The city was built right up to the shores of the sea, from which wide boulevards led inland to attractive and spacious markets. A huge dyke was created to connect the city with the island of Pharos, where later would stand the

lighthouse which was one of the Seven Wonders of the World. Alexander himself planned the location of the many temples and shrines and which Greek and Egyptian gods they would honor.

Legend has it that when it came time to draw the boundaries of the city, no suitable chalk could be found, so the architect and his assistants used seeds and grains, which they sprinkled along the ground to delineate the city's outline. When they finished, a flock of birds rose out of the Nile delta and swooped down, devouring the grain. This at first greatly distressed Alexander, but his seers considered the matter and all were in agreement with Aristander's interpretation that in actuality this was a sign of great good fortune, for the city which would rise on that site would be a source of nourishment of all kinds for its inhabitants and neighbors. When Alexander heard this he ordered that construction begin without delay.

God or Man?

Alexander ordered his naval fleet to sail up the Nile to the capital city of Memphis. Setting out on foot with his armies, he proceeded southward along the eastern bank of the river. Along the route, the natives received him with respect and he encountered no conflicts along the way. They passed the site of the Great Pyramids and the Sphinx, marveling at how different was Egypt than any of the other worlds Alexander had seen and conquered. Arriving in Heliopolis, he boarded a vessel which ferried him across the river to Memphis.

The priests of Memphis greeted him as he disembarked and hailed him not only as King, but as a god. Since Egyptian custom held that a Pharaoh was also a deity. Alexander made a sacrifice to Apis, the Egyptian bull god. While in Memphis, athletic games and literary contests, as well as entertaining shows were held. The best Greek performers were sent to Egypt for these events.

Alexander very much desired to make a pilgrimage to the shrine of Ammon, in Libya. Two of the most important Greek legendary heroes, Perseus and Heracles, were supposed to have consulted the oracle at the shrine of Ammon, which was believed to be infallible in its accuracy. Alexander fancied himself a descendant of both heroes, believing they all had the blood of Zeus in their veins. Alexander very much wanted some validation to his feeling that he was indeed a god, or at least a son of gods. He hoped the oracle at Ammon could shed light on this question once and for all. Alexander may also have wished the god's approval of his campaign so far and a blessing for his continued adventures.

The journey to the shrine entailed marching hundreds of miles through parched dessert. There was an occasional oasis and it rained quite frequently, but the trek was a difficult, tiring, walk in deep sand through almost completely uninhabited territory. The terrain was completely barren – not a tree or flowering plant decorated the landscape and there were few hills or natural outcroppings of land. The men found it hard to keep their bearings since their footsteps were alternately blown away by the wind, or washed away by the rain. Even Alexander's own scouts despaired of guiding the troops, putting them in a very dangerous situation in an unfamiliar environment. Even the toughest and most seasoned Macedonian warriors in Alexander's entourage began to complain at this seemingly futile hike in the dessert. There was general discontent among the troops for the first time since Alexander's crossing of the Hellespont.

At a point when all seemed lost, Alexander was seemingly saved by the gods who sent him animals to guide him. One version of these events has it that two snakes appeared before the men, and hissing loudly, they pointed the way. Another version says they were crows who guided the armies from above. Either way, Alexander was certain that this was divine assistance and ordered his guides to follow the animals who indeed led them directly to the oracle.

The Oracle of Ammon was in the midst of a vast green oasis of thick flowering plants, fruit trees, and palms. The dessert surrounding this oasis is completely dry, but the site of the temple to this day receives dew in the morning and has a fresh bubbling spring of clear, cold, fresh water in the center. The water was cold during the daylight hours and inexplicably warmed during the evening. Alexander and his men revived themselves with in this amazing spring before presenting themselves to the priests of the Oracle.

Alexander explained to the priests that he had made the perilous journey in search of truth. He was instructed to enter and present his queries alone.

Alexander approached and entered the temple unaccompanied. He first asked whether the murder of his father, King Philip, had been properly avenged. The answer came that yes, Philip's killers had been punished. Greatly relieved, Alexander put his second, most burning question to the oracle. When he emerged from the temple, Alexander announced that he had his answer. An unmistakable and clear voice had told him that he was indeed the son of Zeus Ammon, which meant that he himself was a god.

Alexander was of course most pleased with the answers he'd been given by the oracle. It confirmed what Olympias had so often tried to impress upon him, and it brought him closer still to the heroes of Homer, thoughts of whom never left him for more than an instant. He tried to be modest so as not to appear too proud in front of his companions. Many times the King was heard to say that yes, a god was his father, "But is not gods the fathers of all men?" He even tried to downplay the significance of this revelation, telling people his blood was red as any man's and that he felt pain when wounded in battle. There is no doubt however, that Alexander was influenced by the "knowledge" that he was divine, and this was noticed and sometimes scoffed at by his men. Alexander himself would sometimes lament, especially when events turned unexpected or tragic, that being a god seemed to help him very little.

The Prince of Persia is not Born

Throughout the journeys of Alexander's armies, his female prisoners, the family of Darius, had been treated with the utmost respect and dignity. The King made sure they traveled in comfort and granted their every request. When it became apparent that Statira, Darius' wife was in advanced pregnancy, the physician Philip was assigned to look after her. Even with the best of care, however, it soon became clear that the birth was to be a dangerous one, with the child positioned poorly in the womb. Statira labored for a long time, with the encouragement of her own mother and Philip, but in the end, her strength gave way, and she died along with her unborn prince. Alexander mourned the queen genuinely and provided her a stately royal funeral.

Darius received the news of his wife's death from emissaries who escaped Alexander's camp and rode urgently to alert their King. Darius was beside himself with grief, and cursed Alexander fiercely. The messengers however, begged an audience with the King, and when they described the realities of captivity under Alexander, Darius paid rapt attention. He listened as they described the treatment his wife, daughters, and mother received. He heard that Alexander never touched his wife, never compromised her modesty in any way, and had surrounded her with admiration and consideration. The men did not stop at Alexander's care for the prisoners. They regaled Darius with Alexander's qualities as a man – his honesty, courage, and nobility.

Darius was deeply and profoundly moved by what he was told. Bursting into tears, he raised his hands to the heaven and prayed that should it come to pass that the gods would have him lose his throne, that his successor be none other than Alexander.

Alexander Leaves Egypt

The army made its way back to Memphis in the spring of 331 B.C., and Alexander was hailed as Pharaoh and given highest Egyptian honors. Alexander had been very impressed with Egypt, and they would most certainly not forget him. Work continued in Alexandria, and by the time Alexander's body was brought back for burial there, it would be an imposing city indeed. It was time now, however, for Alexander and his troops to turn back to the east. A bridge was built to span the Nile, and they then crossed over and began the long march back to Phoenicia. The navy had been sent ahead to meet them in Tyre where Alexander let his armies rest and take part in athletic games and religious ceremonies held in honor of Heracles.

Diplomatic and political matters were attended to while the armies were idle in Tyre. A ship arrived from Athens carrying representatives requesting a conference with the King. They brought the news that the Spartans, the only Greeks who did not support Alexander, were again planning some kind of resistance. Alexander send Amphoterus to deal with the Spartan threat, and in the end granted the Athenians all of their requests, including the release of thousands of Athenian prisoners taken at the Battle of Granicus.

Alexander appointed his trusted general Ptolemy to his personal bodyguard, and Harpalus was made treasurer. He appointed governors of the areas west of Taurus, of Phoenicia, and of Syria. Antipater sent emissaries to keep Alexander informed of matters under his administration in Macedonia.

When at last he felt that the lands he had already conquered were in good hands, Alexander was ready to get his troops on the march once again. The time had come to push eastward into Persian territory and deal with Darius once and for all. The armies were well rested and trained, and morale was extremely high after the respite and games of Tyre.

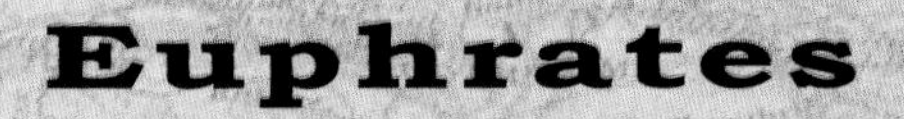

Euphrates

Darius had not been idly waiting for Alexander to come after him. When he realized that his offers of truce with the Macedonian would never be accepted, he resigned himself to the necessity of fighting, and fight he would, believing until the last that he had a chance to redeem himself as King of Kings. Darius had certainly come to fear, and perhaps even to respect Alexander, but he was far from ready to give up, and wished to reverse his humiliation at Issus.

While Alexander and his armies rested at Tyre over the summer, Darius began to hope that they had tired and perhaps were losing the desire to continue. Nothing could have been further from the truth, of course, but with Alexander busy with administration of his empire and overseeing games and entertainments, Darius' began to feel he had a true fighting chance over the younger King.

Alexander was ready to begin the eastward push in July of 331 B.C. He sent Hephaestion with a sizeable force toward the Euphrates River. They marched for a week until they reached the thriving commercial center at Thepsacus, a city built on the bank. Pausing there, Hephaestion took stock of the situation, and saw that the deep overflowing river could not be forged by horses or on foot. It was apparent that only bridges would get the troops across, and he ordered construction to begin at once. No sooner had the work started than a Darius' general Mazaeus appeared on the opposite bank with a force of nearly three thousand men. Many of these were Greek Mercenaries, ready to fight tooth and nail against their own countrymen. Mazaeus' men harassed and attacked Hephaestion's builders but work was steady on the bridges nonetheless.

Meanwhile, Alexander and the rest of his armies set out from Tyre, arriving in Thepsacus in August. When they arrived Alexander was greeted with the sight of two hefty bridges, almost completed, spanning the Euphrates. The moment Mazaeus saw Alexander approach from the other side of the river, he turned and fled with his men, allowing the bridges to be completed quickly, and the troops to cross over undisturbed. Alexander marched his men through Mesopotamia, along the river, taking prisoners along the way – mostly defectors from Darius' camp. These prisoners provided vital information on Darius' plans and intentions and the state of his forces. They reported the Darius had built up an army far greater even than he'd had at Issus. They estimated that he already had over one million men under his command. Darius had no intention of repeating his tactical errors of Issus. This time he was determined to face off with Alexander in an open plain with plenty of room for his chariots and cavalry to maneuver and where the enormity of his armies would be a decided advantage.

Alexander was not deterred by the news of Darius' tremendous force. In fact the knowledge that the great battle was soon at hand raised his energy and he spurred his troops to greater speed as they made their way onward toward the Tigris River. From the point where the Macedonians had crossed the Euphrates, the Tigris ran almost parallel some fifty miles to the east. Alexander fully expected Darius and his armies to be staring them down from the opposite bank of the river, and mentally the men were prepared for a difficult crossing. As it happened, when they arrived at the river there was no enemy in sight. The only opposition they encountered when forging the Tigris was the fierce current which buffeted men, horses, and wagons about in the deep water as the heavily armored troops pushed through the water. They thanked good fortune that the enemy was not present when utterly exhausted, they reassembled. Alexander allowed a brief respite after the river crossing, and took the opportunity to offer sacrifices so as to keep the gods on his side during the coming danger. Just as he finished the sacrificial ceremony, the amazed armies witnessed a total eclipse of the moon. The King had no doubt that such an event was a message meant expressly for him, and he called Aristander to give him the interpretation of this astonishing sign. The seer pronounced the eclipse a

sure sign that the sacrifices had been received with appreciation and that within one month Alexander would win a major and decisive victory.

Alexander guided his troops along the eastern shores of the Tigris and day after day they saw no sign of the enemy. On the fourth day the Macedonian scouts came back with a report; a Persian force was just ahead in an open field, lying in wait for Alexander. Darius was not among them, however, and they were but a small fraction of his men, perhaps one thousand strong. Alexander maneuvered his battalions into fighting form and readied for battle as they pressed on, not certain that the estimation of the number of Persians they would encounter would really be so unthreatening. They indeed came upon Persian cavalry and charged for them with Alexander in the fore. The King's telltale white plumes waved as he rode at the front of the Royal Squadron, with the rest of the army closely following. The Persians gave up immediately without a fight. Turning on their heels, they desperately bolted for their lives. Alexander's men took off in hot pursuit and captured many of the fleeing Persians, but just as many escaped. The prisoners supplied the information that Alexander had been waiting for: Darius' and his million man force were situated just a few days' march away. The Persians outnumbered them by at least five men to one.

The Battle of Gaugamela

Hearing that Darius was truly close by, Alexander decided to give his troops another much needed rest before the final showdown. He ordered the building of a secure camp and the men stayed put for four days before setting out again only lightly armed and prepared to maneuver easily in a wide open setting. As they passed over a slight rise, they caught sight of Darius' army a few miles away, near Gaugamela, in a great open plain. From their vantage point on high they saw the layout of the Persian forces. Parmenio advised Alexander to halt the troops for the time being and watch the enemy to assess their strategy. A meeting was called of all officers and staff to apprise them of the plans of action. Alexander mounted Bucephalus, and facing his trusted generals and commanders, he made an impassioned speech. The young King reminded his leaders what was in store, and what was at stake. Babylon itself lay just over the horizon. Who would be sovereign of the continent of Asia would be decided in this decisive campaign. Morale was high, and the men expressed confidence in their chief and pride in their mission.

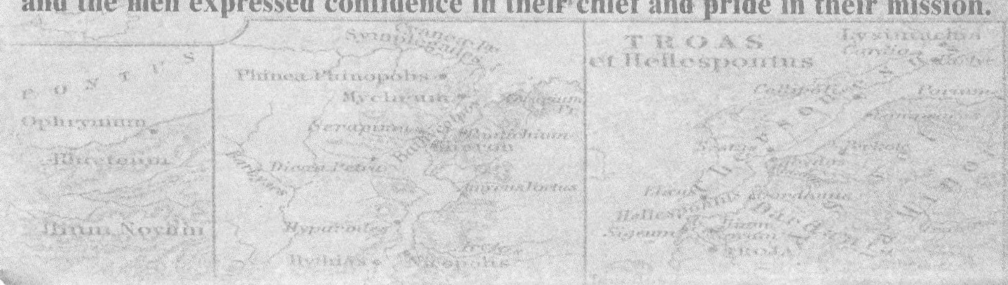

When at last the battle was imminent, Parmenio discussed timing with Alexander, pointing out that a night attack would give them the advantage, and suggesting they charge the enemy camp while they slept. Alexander dismissed this suggestion as cowardly and unseemly for a mighty conqueror such as himself. He declared he would win his battles in daylight, giving his enemies full opportunity to defend themselves. He would be victorious by force and by wit, and he would never stoop to "stealing victory". Alexander set the battle to begin at dawn, and proceeded to sleep soundly that night, while Darius and his soldiers nervously guarded their sleepless camp, worried that Alexander would attempt the very thing he had refused to contemplate.

Not only did Alexander sleep well the night before the battle; he slept quite a bit later than usual. When at last his men found the courage to rouse him he simply declared that he was tired from planning the day's fighting. He displayed a complete and utter confidence that things would play out exactly as he

planned. Certainly planning was necessary and nothing less than brilliant strategy would assure victory against such enormous odds. The Persian cavalry alone numbered some thirty five thousand, against Alexander's seven thousand. The terrain was ideal for Darius' beloved chariots and for his plentiful infantry. But Alexander's sleep had been sound, as his strategy and leadership would prove to be.

Darius struck first. His cavalry attacked Alexander's right wing. While Alexander's smaller force held off thousands upon thousands of Persian cavalry, Darius sent in his chariots. These were easily picked off by Alexander's men who slaughtered the horses and drivers alike. The fighting was hard and furious. Alexander about one hundred men, and many more were wounded, including Hephaestion. Once again the phalanx proved invaluable, as did the training and precision of the Macedonian army, along with the leadership and cool-headed command of its generals. Alexander drove a wedge into Darius' right flank, causing the Persian

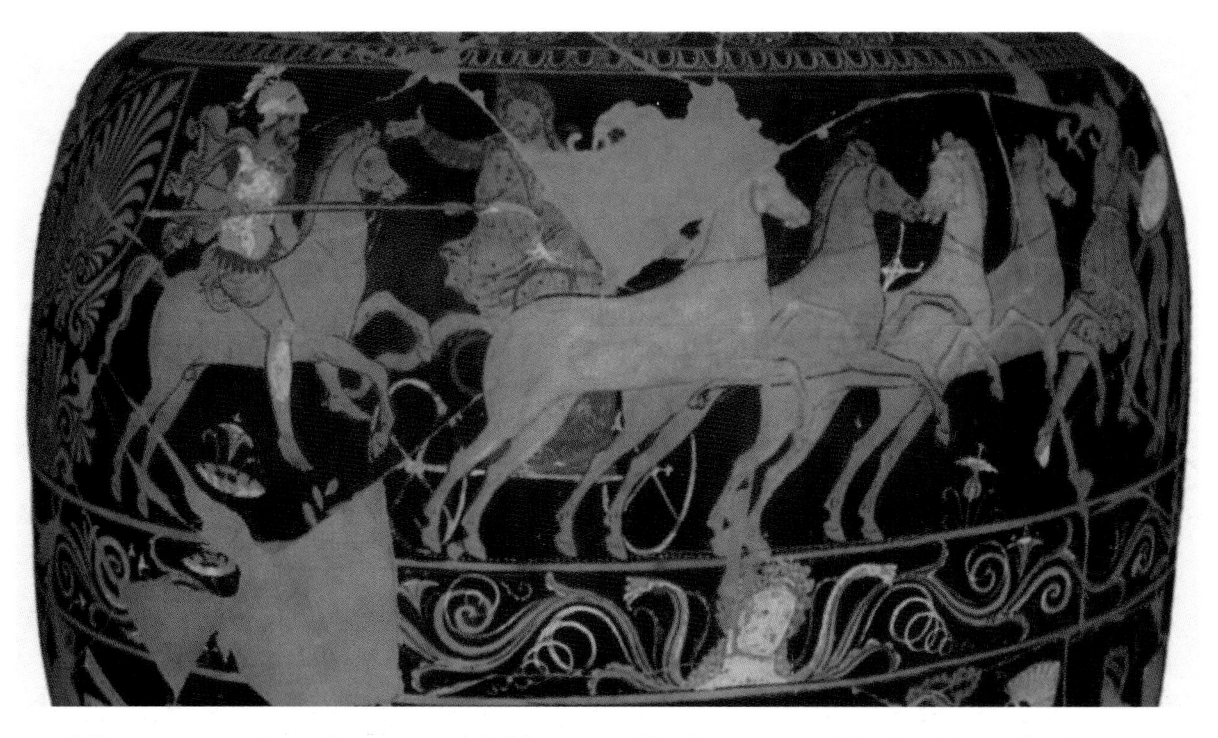

general Bessus to panic and retreat with his men. Darius, meanwhile, had been in the center of his forces, along with his entourage and found himself cut off from his armies. The great King did just what he had done at the battle of Issus. He ran for his life, abandoning the thousands of men who were still fighting and dying for him.

The Persian army fell into complete disarray, and withdrew. Alexander ordered an all-out pursuit, and with the King himself leading, they chased the Persians all the following night. Thousands upon thousands of Darius' men were massacred. The one man Alexander wanted most to capture or kill, however, once again had escaped his grasp. He and his various companions and attendants had kept up their flight without stopping even to destroy bridges behind them, until they reached Arbela, where they were joined by several of Darius' fleeing generals and many of his troops. By the time Alexander reached Arbela however, Darius had vanished. He had abandoned his chariot, his bow, and his treasure, which was quite a substantial booty for Alexander. The battle of Gaugamela had been won, just as Aristander had foretold.

After Alexander gave up the chase, Darius continued eastward along with a few thousand loyal survivors. He still had not given up all hope of raising another army to face Alexander another day. He knew that Alexander and his men would now make straight for Babylon, and he hoped they would lose themselves in the pleasures of the flesh and the luxurious lifestyle they would find there.

Alexander did indeed proceed along the Royal Road to Babylon. He kept his armies in battle formation, lest they be met with resistance at gates of the great city. There was no need for such precaution. The Persian governor of Babylon, along with his administrators and

ministers greeted Alexander as King and he marched his men through the streets in triumph. Alexander offered sacrifices to the Babylonian gods, and took possession of the city's considerable treasure. The Macedonian armies took up residence in Babylon for a time of rest and recreation, allowing the women of Babylon to afford them some pleasures of which they had not tasted for quite some time.

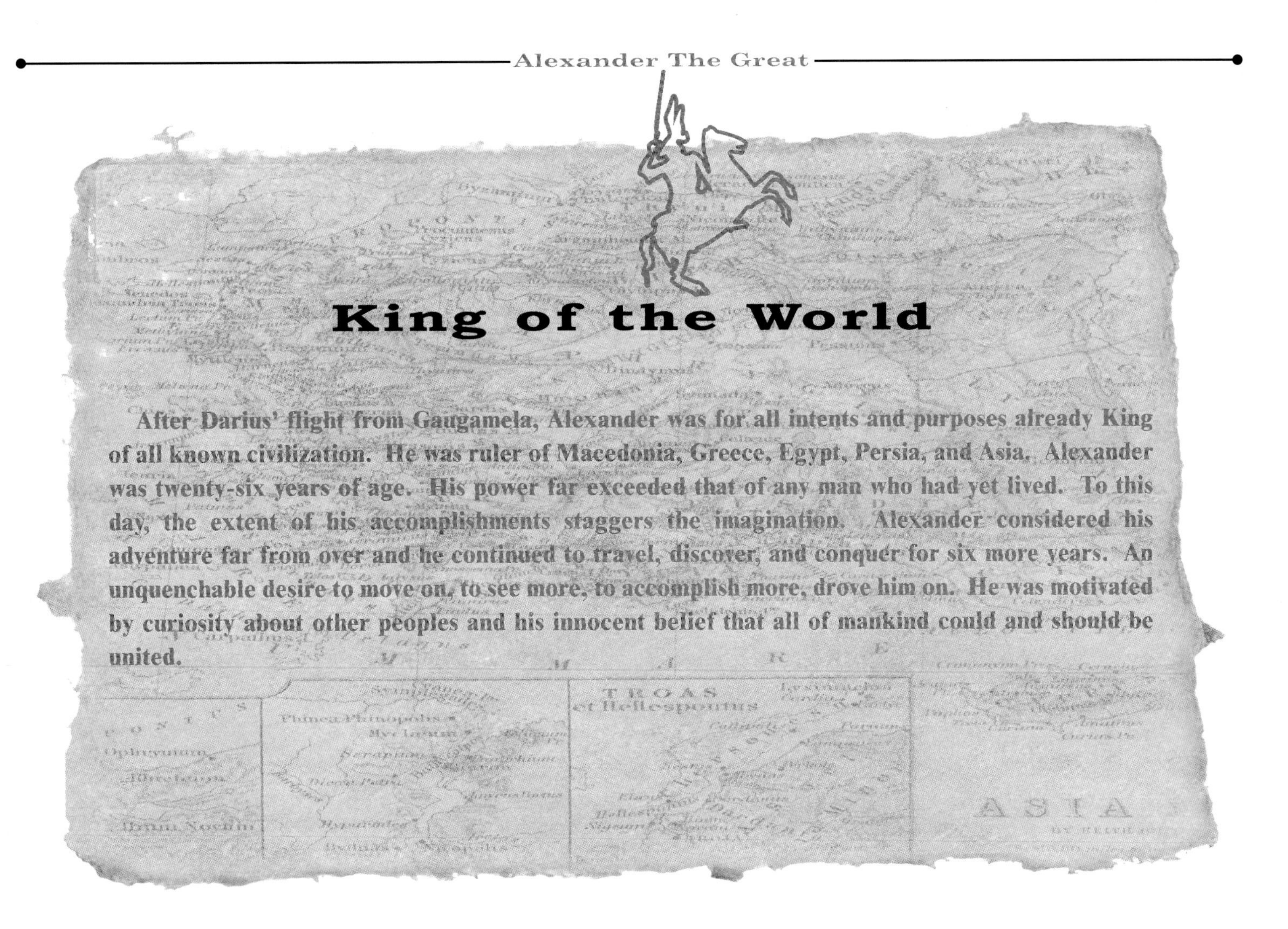

King of the World

After Darius' flight from Gaugamela, Alexander was for all intents and purposes already King of all known civilization. He was ruler of Macedonia, Greece, Egypt, Persia, and Asia. Alexander was twenty-six years of age. His power far exceeded that of any man who had yet lived. To this day, the extent of his accomplishments staggers the imagination. Alexander considered his adventure far from over and he continued to travel, discover, and conquer for six more years. An unquenchable desire to move on, to see more, to accomplish more, drove him on. He was motivated by curiosity about other peoples and his innocent belief that all of mankind could and should be united.

And what of Alexander the young man? Stories have been passed down for generations about the character of the amazing King. In most of these anecdotes Alexander is kind, compassionate, and even wise. One story goes that as he and his men were traveling wearily in a dry dessert, on their chase after Darius, they and their horses suffered from a mighty thirst. They came upon a band of men carrying water over the dunes. The men recognized Alexander and approached him, offering the King and his men a drink. When questioned it came to light that the men had wandered for days searching for water to bring back to their children, but they were willing to give the water to Alexander instead. The men were sent on to their children – not a drop of their water was accepted, and Alexander and his men continued their weary and thirsty trek.

Throughout his travels, Alexander showed the utmost kindness to his men who were wounded in battle or who fell ill on the journey. Many were sent home to Greece and Macedonia to recuperate. One of Alexander's officers, Eurylochus, petitioned for repatriation, claiming to be suffering some ailment which incapacitated him for duty. On investigation, Alexander discovered that the officer suffered from no illness other than lovesickness, and that the object of his love, Telesippa, was slated to set out for Greece. Alexander was not angry at the effort at deception, and desired to right the situation for the better of all concerned. He called for Eurylochus and advised him that his request to be sent home was denied, since he would not sent away under false pretenses. Alexander went on to add that neither would he force Telesippa to leave, as she was a free woman and could do as she pleased. He advised Eurylochus to try to make Telesippa choose to stay with him, using the power of his own love. Alexander's counsel was taken to heart, and the pair remained in Asia together.

Even back in far away Macedonia, Alexander's reputation for generosity and loyalty to friends was known. Olympias was not pleased, and in her many letters to her son she rebuked him for over-spending and warned him that his friends would someday betray them if he didn't watch his back. Olympias took her complaints to Antipater, who notified Alexander, but there was little the King could do from so far off to quell his mother's outbursts. His mother's letters were a secret known only to himself and his dear friend Hephaestion.

Aristotle, too, kept in touch with his powerful student. Alexander had added all sorts of people from a wide range of professions to his entourage, and reported on their research to his mentor. He told him of the natural phenomena and the many sociological observations which he knew would interest his old teacher. Their correspondence was not limited to academics, however. Aristotle even provided suggestions for winning battles and for political changes in the areas Alexander conquered.

Perhaps it was Aristotle's influence then, which was behind Alexander's revolutionary management of the new lands. He set about to decentralize the Persian Empire, appointing many local governors, of Persian, Greek, and Macedonian extraction. The

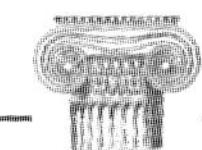

Alexander the Invincible

In eight years of campaigning throughout the known world of his time, Alexander never lost a single battle. Not once did his armies not emerge victorious! Hundreds, perhaps thousands of communities of all kinds surrendered to him with no combat whatsoever. Some welcomed him as conquering hero. Many of the finest armies fled in fear as Alexander approached. Interspersed among these easy conquests raged difficult battles where Alexander's men had to fight tooth and nail while sustaining painful losses, and even sieges which took months to subdue a particularly proud populace, but these were by far the minority and Alexander ultimately prevailed each and every time.

people took well to this system, commenting that where Darius had been just one, now there were "many Alexanders".

Babylon indeed proved a soft and luxurious resting place for the weary Macedonians. The months they tarried there spoiled them to some extent. Many of the men began to wear the decorative outfits of the Orient, to enjoy anointing themselves with perfume, and generally to succumb to the decadence which then characterized the East. The armies began to replace their toughness with a certain laxness and softness which their leader abhorred. Alexander himself tried to avoid temptation and went out of his way to demonstrate his athletic prowess and his strength. On one occasion, when representatives of Sparta arrived in Babylon on an official visit, Alexander impressed them by fighting a duel with a lion, and winning!

One hundred percent success no doubt fed Alexander's view of himself as invincible. Certainly many others considered him so, among his own men as among his rivals. He never showed hesitation in the face of danger, leading his men at the front of the battle lines, setting an example of fearlessness and valor. While military custom of the time dictated that a general placed himself at the front lines, rather than directing from the sidelines or behind the scenes, Alexander was particularly courageous and always made himself visible in the thick of battle. When his armies encountered a fortress or walled city, it was invariably Alexander who was the first to storm the barricades.

Alexander may have been invincible, but he was made of flesh and blood after all. He sustained many wounds, some of them quite serious. In the Battle of Granicus he sustained a horrible gash in the head and neck wounds in hand to hand combat, making a narrow escape with his life. At Issus he was stabbed through his thigh. At Gaza he received shoulder and ankle

Into Persia

But let us return to the adventure. Alexander decided his men had taken their fill of the luxuries of Babylon, and turned his troops toward Susa, the administrative seat of the Persian Empire. The Macedonian armies again formed battle units and marched for three weeks toward the glittering city which was the site of tremendous riches. While on their way, messengers arrived bearing welcoming greetings from Susa, and promises that Alexander would be hailed as King and would receive the treasure forthwith. A small delegation had already arrived ahead of the armies and reported that all was well and the treasure, which was in the royal palace, had been seized. The riches the city yielded forth were even more than had been supposed. Along with fifty thousand talents of silver (an amount worth what today

wounds, and his lung was pierced straight through in India. Each time Alexander was hurt he put his trust in his physicians, never doubted that he would recover fully, and always rallied in short order, ready for the next challenge.

The unstoppable, the insurmountable, the completely indomitable Alexander won and won again, until his armies simply ran out of emotional steam and stopped. Alexander the Great died young, but unbeaten.

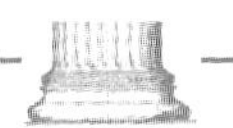

would be the equivalent of hundreds of millions of dollars) there were bronze statues which Alexander had sent back to Greece and which graced the Acropolis. Legend has it that over twenty thousand mules and five thousand camels had to be employed to carry the vast treasure that Susa showered on the King. Alexander in turn showered his men with lavish gifts from the bounty they had received. While in Susa, the Macedonians oversaw athletic contests and festivals, and Alexander of course paid homage to the gods and offered the traditional sacrifices.

At around this time, Antipater, back home in Macedonia, had a dangerous situation to contend with, and he sent urgent notices to the King for assistance. Sparta, the only Greek state still in opposition to Alexander, had launched an attempt to overthrow Macedonian rule in Greece. The Spartan King, Agis II, believed that Alexander had ventured so far eastward that he had lost his control over the home front, leaving it vulnerable. Nothing could have been further from the truth, however, and Antipater handled the crisis well, with his King's support from afar. Alexander sent his navy home to support Antipater's forces, and a huge sum of money to be used to finance the war against Sparta. Antipater and the home army crushed the rebellion, and effectively ended Sparta's days as a military power. Alexander dismissed many of his Greek fighters, fearing for the unity of his forces and their loyalty to him.

After Susa was secured, Persian governors appointed and a tax system in place, Alexander began his push into Persia proper. They began to march in a southeastern direction, through Uxian country. The people in the plains surrendered readily to Alexander and they made quick progress toward the mountainous terrain to the east. When they reached the high areas, however, the disposition of the natives changed. These Uxians were accustomed to liberty, and indeed had never recognized Persian sovereignty over them.

The Great King Darius himself had been forced to pay tolls for safe passage through this land, which he had never really ruled. The same was now expected from Alexander. As Alexander approached, he received messages from the hill people that he would be expected to ransom himself and his men.

Alexander told the messengers that he would meet representatives of the Uxians at the mountain pass, and would give them what they asked. Perhaps he was anxious to reach Persia and had no patience for this obstacle, or perhaps he was getting older and bending his principles to fit the times. Whatever the reason, Alexander decided on a tactic which he previously had deplored. He led his soldiers quickly off in an unexpected direction, from which they came upon the Uxians unawares, swooping into their villages and killing many in their

beds. After overpowering the villagers he proceeded to the pass to meet the delegation which would exact his pay. His forces seized the pass in one swipe, and the waiting Uxians took hasty flight. It was clear that it was the natives who would pay dues to Alexander, and not the other way around.

Darius' mother begged an audience with Alexander at this juncture, and beseeched him to allow the Uxian people to return peacefully to their homes and retain their territory in return for a tribute to be paid to the King. Alexander gave in to this request, the people were given their villages back, and the tax was set at a number of sheep and horses to be paid annually.

Revenge or Benevolence?

Alexander ordered Parmenio to lead the troops onto the main road into Persia. They made their way through the hills with as much speed as possible for sixty thousand armored troops and cavalry. Their destination: Persepolis, the golden city of Persia. While still in the mountainous territory the Macedonians were met with a defensive force consisting of thousands of troops and hundreds of horses, sent to deny them access to the pass which led to Persepolis. Alexander halted his advance for one day while he considered how to meet this predicament. The very next day, he ordered his armies to push straight through the resistance, and they proceeded, under fire of missiles and arrows, losing many troops to death and injury. They managed to capture indigenous prisoners, however, who proved invaluable as sources of information about the area. The prisoners led Alexander along an alternate route to the pass over difficult and rocky terrain, where the Persians would not expect they would travel. Moving under cover of darkness, they managed to catch the enemy by surprise and took the pass against no real resistance.

The King of Asia now began to suffer some psychological setbacks which perhaps mark the slow beginning of his end. Alexander marched into Persepolis with revenge in his heart. Still preoccupied with the invasion of Greece by the Persians some one hundred and fifty years previous, Alexander was intent on avenging the deeds of Xerxes, and believed the present citizens of Persepolis to be placed there to receive the punishment. On the one hand, he wished to rule Persia, and indeed the world, benevolently and respectfully, while on the other hand he saw himself as a vengeful god, whose purpose was to exact the price, which as he saw it, the people owed.

Alexander's loyal and trustworthy older general, Parmenio, counseled his young leader to check his vengeful impulses and to spare the edifices of Persepolis, which in any case were now the King's own property. Alexander rejected his advice, and burned the great palace of the Persian Kings to the ground. He reminded Parmenio of the destruction in Athens of temples and shrines at the hand of Xerxes and insisted that this was just retribution.

The Macedonian soldiers as a whole remained loyal to Alexander during this period, as always. There were, however, the beginnings of grumblings and feelings of dissatisfaction. Perhaps the purpose of the adventure had become blurred, or perhaps the men were simply exhausted after over three years of fighting far from home. Many wanted to end the wars and return to Greece. They saw no purpose to pushing further east. After all, Alexander had already toppled the mighty Persian Empire and was now the undisputed ruler as far as their imaginations could carry them. Furthermore, Alexander had added thirty thousand Persian forces to his armies, a move which was not well received among his seasoned Macedonian troops, and which threatened the cohesiveness of the fighting force. When the men saw the temple burning they let up a cheer, assuming this meant the end of the wars and signaled their return home. Seeing that morale had begun to suffer serious damage, and Alexander mounted a campaign of speeches and orations meant to return him the loyalty of his forces and to motivate them for next eastward trek. To a large extent he was successful, but complaining and malcontent among the troops never really ended after this point, and later, as we will see, grew ever more insistent.

The End of Darius

Word was brought to Alexander that Darius had reached Media and had taken up residence there until such time that the Macedonians would again be on the march. Alexander had had enough of the Persian King and his immediate objective was to finally capture him. The armies left Persepolis and within twelve days they had reached Media. Darius was already in retreat however, so Alexander pressed on after him. He pushed his armies to greater and greater speed, until many of his men simply dropped out and horses were dropping dead in their tracks. Alexander kept pushing forward regardless of these losses, and reached Rhagae after eleven days. They were now only a day's march from the Caspian Gates, but Darius and his motley army had already passed through. Realizing this, Alexander halted his men and allowed them to rest. Many of Darius' men who had deserted the Persian forces found their way to the Macedonian camp, surrendered to Alexander and supplied strategic information. While they rested, Alexander took care of political matters in Media, appointing a Persian governor.

When they were once again on the move, Alexander marched his armies through the Caspian Gates, and shortly thereafter received two messengers claiming to have urgent news. They reported that Darius had been captured by his own men! Nabarzanes, Darius' cavalry commander, his general Bessus and other officers had forcibly seized their King and held him under arrest. Bessus was now in command of the Persian cavalry and all other Persians who had been with Darius as he retreated. Bessus claimed the right to take over the power of the captive King on the basis of his familial relationship to Darius, and because Darius had succumbed in Bessus' own home province. Only the Greek mercenaries remained loyal to the Persian King and took off on their own into the hills.

Alexander knew no time must be lost. He appointed Craterus, who had become one of his closest and most trusted confidants as well as an

accomplished general, in charge of the main body of the army and ordered him to arrange the troops in war formation, ready to follow behind. Alexander set off immediately with great haste, taking with him a small force consisting of the King's Companions, some of his toughest light infantrymen, and scouts. They carried only their personal weapons and two days' supplies. Speed was of the essence.

Marching at full press for two days, they arrived at the camp where the informants had said Darius had been seized. It was empty – there was no sign of the enemy. Alexander allowed no delay, and continued his pursuit at full throttle, driving his men and horses almost to the limit of their endurance. They marched through the night until they reached a village where Darius and his captors had bee the previous day. Here they learned of a dangerous path which they could use as a shortcut.

This route was without water and totally uninhabited, but Alexander insisted on taking off immediately, ordering the native informants to come along as guides.

Alexander insisted on moving with great speed, and at one point his infantrymen were so exhausted he ordered his cavalrymen to dismount and give them their horses. They covered over fifty miles in the course of one night, and at the break of dawn were greeted with the sight of the Persians. Their force was a straggling and unmotivated parade. They offered only light resistance, and as soon as Alexander himself approached most of them fled.

Bessus and a few others tried to make off with Darius in his covered wagon, but when they saw Alexander coming, two of Bessus' men fell on their King and mortally stabbed him.

Darius managed to speak only a few more words, and with these he beseeched his assassins to embrace Alexander and thank him for his treatment of his family. The killers escaped on horseback just before Alexander arrived at the covered wagon. When he entered, Alexander found his enemy dead in a pool of blood. Reverently, he closed Darius' eyelids, and taking off his cloak, he covered the body with hit.

And so the King of Kings finally found his end. In death, the fifty year old Darius was perhaps more fortunate than in life. Alexander sent his body back to Persepolis, and afforded him a royal funeral and burial in the royal tombs.

His family was treated exactly as they would have been had Darius remained King, and Alexander looked after the education of his children as befit the offspring of a monarch.

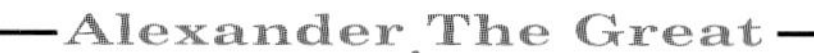

Changes

When the Macedonian troops heard that Darius was dead, a great cheer went up among the throngs. Most of Alexander's soldiers assumed that this spelled the absolute end of the war, and that they now would be going home. Once again, Alexander had to contend with the misconception among his armies as to the purpose and extent of the adventure of which they were a part. Alexander had apparently never made clear exactly what his final objective was. Perhaps he did not have a clear idea himself of what he was after – he only knew he was not finished with this mighty expedition. He was young, and there were certainly more worlds to conquer! Most of the men were loyal to Alexander and ready and willing to continue the journey. A growing group of dissenters however, was making itself known. Ironically, as Alexander seemed to lean more and more toward the idea that he was indeed a deity, the men seemed to see him as ever more mortal and fallible. Alexander's behavior became erratic, and he drank more often into a state of inebriation. One night Alexander as banqueted with his officers he became embroiled in an argument with Cleitus, "The Black", his close friend and confidant. Some Persians had insulted the Macedonians and Cleitus had risen up to defend his countrymen. A violent drunken brawl ensued, during which Cleitus furiously protested the fact that the Orientals present were making fun of the Europeans. Alexander accused Cleitus of stirring up trouble and called Cleitus a coward. Cleitus faced the King and declared that he had betrayed Macedonia by denouncing Philip as his father and claiming the god Zeus-Ammon instead. At this, Alexander became enraged, and charged at his friend. Onlookers who feared bloodshed grabbed Alexander's sword away from him, but he took one from the nearest guard and rammed it through Cleitus' body. This was the same Cleitus who had been his treasured comrade and confidant, and who had saved Alexander's own life in the battle of Granicus! Alexander was remorseful almost to the point of suicide when he realized what he had done, and lay on the ground grieving, refusing to take water or food. After several days like this, he rose and made sacrifices to the gods asking forgiveness for his heinous deed and seemed to recover. After this, even those closest to him feared his temperamental and unpredictable behavior.

Alexander felt that in his new role as King of Asia he needed to court the respect and understanding of the eastern people. He seemed to disregard the fact that the Macedonians in his entourage chafed under the new order. He took to wearing Persian clothing such as was traditionally worn by their Kings, and discarded his former simple Macedonian dress. The King surrounded himself with a formal court, replacing his previous openness and comradery. The new court was replete with pomp and circumstance, and all those coming into the presence of Alexander were required to prostrate themselves at his feet, an act which recognized his divinity, according to Persian tradition. Many Persians were inducted into Alexander's armies, including the brother of Darius who entered the ranks of the elite Companions.

All of this served to take him down in the eyes of his followers. So serious was the dissent in some circles that a plot to kill Alexander was hatched. Philotas, son of Parmenio, was accused of masterminding the plot. Philotas and Alexander had been friends since early childhood, and Philotas was known as a valiant and loyal commander. Of late, however, it seemed he'd been corrupted by the luxurious eastern lifestyle and by his own military success. Rumors of Philotas' betrayal of the King reached Alexander, and he ordered that Philotas and several other officers be tortured to death. When Philotas was dead, Alexander realized that Parmenio would have to be told. He could not bring himself to bring the old general such news, fearing Parmenio would go insane with grief. Philotas had been his last remaining son, after losing two others in battle. Alexander, instead of sending Parmenio a message bearing the horrible truth, he sent an assassin to put Parmenio to death as well.

These events spelled major changes for the Macedonian camp. Urgent messages from Antipater urged Alexander to take stock of his behavior and many observers even feared the King was losing his sanity. Alexander, they felt, was behaving more like a paranoid Persian despot than like the proud Macedonian conqueror they knew him to be.

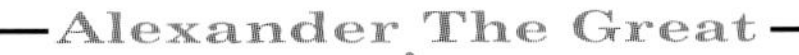

Scythians

Alexander decided it was time to send home the Greek Allied troops that had been so loyal to him during this entire expedition. The deeds of King Xerxes had been avenged, and to Alexander's mind the rest of the adventure was more fitting to a force made up of eastern troops along with the Macedonians. He lavished the departing soldiers with gifts, recognized each one by name and commended those who had distinguished themselves in battle.

The armies looked eastward once again. They approached the country of the Scythians, a people Homer had called "the most righteous of mankind". The Scythians lived in tribal groups, and cherished their independence. They had been at best loosely ruled by the Persian Kings, and did not take to the idea of Alexander's assumption of power in their land. They went on the offensive, seizing Macedonian camps and inciting conflict. Alexander countered their attacks fiercely, sparing no man, woman or child, and plundering anything of value in the Scythian settlements. Town after town was taken, the men slaughtered and the women and children sold into slavery. The largest of the towns was Cyropolis, which had been founded by the great Cyrus. It was a walled city with a comparatively large population which had garrisoned itself inside.

Alexander laid siege to the town without mercy, and when a stream was discovered which ran from outside the walls into the town, he spirited soldiers through the channel who then opened the gates to the rest of the army. The citizens fought furiously and Alexander's men sustained quite a few casualties; Alexander was injured by a boulder thrown at his head, and Craterus was hit by an arrow. Presently however, the town surrendered, and all inhabitants were massacred.

The Macedonians fortified a site near the River Tanais, where Alexander intended to found a city. He envisioned populating it with Greek Mercenaries, local tribesmen who wished to take him up on such an offer, and Macedonians who were no longer fit for military service. While the preparations were made at the site, the Scythians harassed Alexander's men from the opposite bank of the river. Alexander wished to cross the river and take care of them once and for all, but Aristander warned him that the omens did not portend well for a campaign of that sort. Aristander foresaw great danger to Alexander if he continued to come up against the Scythians at that time. Alexander's response to the warning was that he'd rather face any danger than to be humiliated in front of a ridiculous bunch of Scythians. Aristander repeated his warning...

Alexander again used the skin-rafts and moved his men across the river. The battle was heated, and when the Scythians retreated the Macedonians pursued them toward the Jaxartes River. The weather was scorching and the earth was parched, and the soldiers suffered from severe thirst. Alexander himself drank some water which turned out to be contaminated, and he came down with an attack of dysentery. Alexander's illness allowed a window of opportunity for some of the unfortunate Scythians to make their escape, and Alexander was hauled back to camp by Hephaestion in a very bad state. Aristander had been right after all.

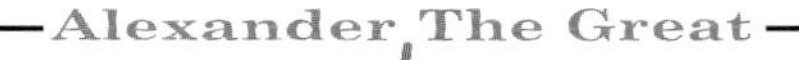

Eastward Ho

Word came back to Alexander that Bessus had proclaimed himself successor to Darius' throne and was calling himself Artixerxes, King of Persia. Alexander was incensed and vowed to bring him to justice in short order. Bessus fled eastward into the vast area of Bactria, torching the fields and laying waste to the land behind him as he went. Alexander set off in pursuit, passing through lands populated with indigenous tribes who fought him fiercely but futilely. After suffering heavy damage these natives reluctantly accepted Alexander's reign, and he founded towns for them, encouraging them to settle down and give up their nomadic existence.

While in Bactria, Alexander captured a local chieftain and his enchantingly beautiful daughter, the dancer Roxane. In the year 328 B.C. Alexander was twenty eight years old when he took Roxane as his first wife. As a matter of fact, as far as we know, this was the first time Alexander had taken any real interest in a woman, and although Roxane was an attractive and talented young lady, many historians believe the marriage made as much for political reasons as for love. Alexander encouraged his men to follow his lead and to take wives from among the local women. He believed that the intermingling of families was the surest way to world unity. Aristotle, it should be noted, advised against this policy, as he believed it would weaken Alexander and Macedonia to treat the conquered peoples as kinsmen, but Alexander ignored his teacher's counsel in this matter.

Alexander was sure that the intermarriage afforded the natives more pride, allowing them to accept him as liberator rather than as subjugator. Then, as family, they would join forces with him as he carried forward his adventure.

Alexander continued his relentless pursuit of Bessus through the winter. He marched his troops through heavy and deep snow without respite. Lack of provisions, cold, and exhaustion dogged the army, but still they pressed on for the Causasus Mountains. Achieving the range, they plied the trails for weeks and when they emerged, weary and hungry from the mountains into the Scythian foothills, they saw that Bessus had destroyed all crops over a wide stretch of the countryside in hopes that lack of food would cause his enemies to turn back. They suffered, but did not cease to move forward, and Bessus was forced to flee farther into Bactria. Alexander easily took the two main cities in the region, Aornos and Batra, which surrendered to him readily. The army continued steadily toward the river Oxus. By the time they reached the water Bessus had already crossed using boats which he burned behind him. Observing the wide raging river with its sandy bottom and the rapid current Alexander understood that only boats or bridges

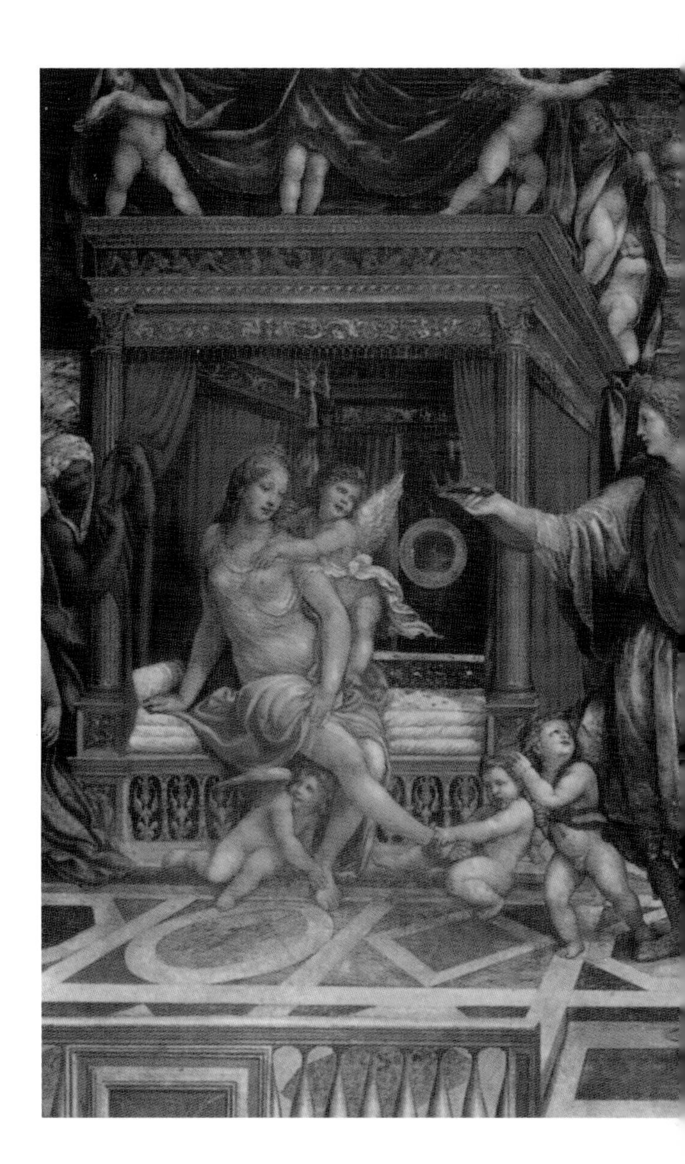

would move the forces across. The land was barren with absolutely no materials available for building bridges. Alexander ordered all of the tents, which were made of hides and pelts, be sown together tightly into sacks, which were filled with dry leaves and other rubbish. These they used as rafts to cross the water. Before the dangerous crossing Alexander discharged all infirm and older soldiers and dispatched them home. With his remaining fit troops he crossed on the cloth rafts in an operation taking five days' time. Once on the other side, they picked up speed and made off in pursuit of Bessus once again.

Word reached Alexander that a mutiny had taken place, and that Bessus was now tasting some of the same medicine he's administered to Darius! Some of Bessus' own people had arrested him and intended to bring turn him over to the Macedonians. Alexander slowed his march and waited for confirmation of these events. Sure enough, messengers arrived saying that Bessus was in custody and that his captures were asking for instructions. Alexander ordered that Bessus be stripped and collared like a dog and brought into his presence. Soon the prisoner appeared before him naked and in stocks. Alexander looked at him with distain, and asked him why he had betrayed and killed Darius, his own King and master. When Bessus replied that he'd done it to save his own skin when it seemed inevitable that Alexander would soon catch up to them, Alexander reacted with loathing and contempt at such cowardice and treachery. He had Bessus brutally flogged and his nose and ears sliced from his body. Later, Bessus was tried by a Persian court and executed by crucifixion.

The fates of Darius and Bessus serve to illustrate to us all of the elements of Alexander's personality and character, and the values which drove him. While Darius, as King of Persia, was Alexander's arch enemy and would be driven from power at all costs, Alexander regretted that he had died an ignoble death at the hands of his own men, and not a heroic one at the hands of his enemies. As we have seen, he afforded Darius a King's send-off, and his family were treated as royalty. Bessus, on the other hand, had committed treachery and even though that was directed at Alexander's own enemy, the act itself compounded by Bessus attempt to usurp the Persian throne was so anathema to Alexander that he punished him with an immense cruelty he reserved only for rare cases.

Soon after these events Alexander endured a disastrous battle against another Scythian tribe, the Spitamenes, which ambushed the Macedonians. There were serious losses and the captured Macedonians were mercilessly butchered. Alexander was greatly grieved by this upset, and set out for revenge. He sped after the Spitamenes, and had them all killed.

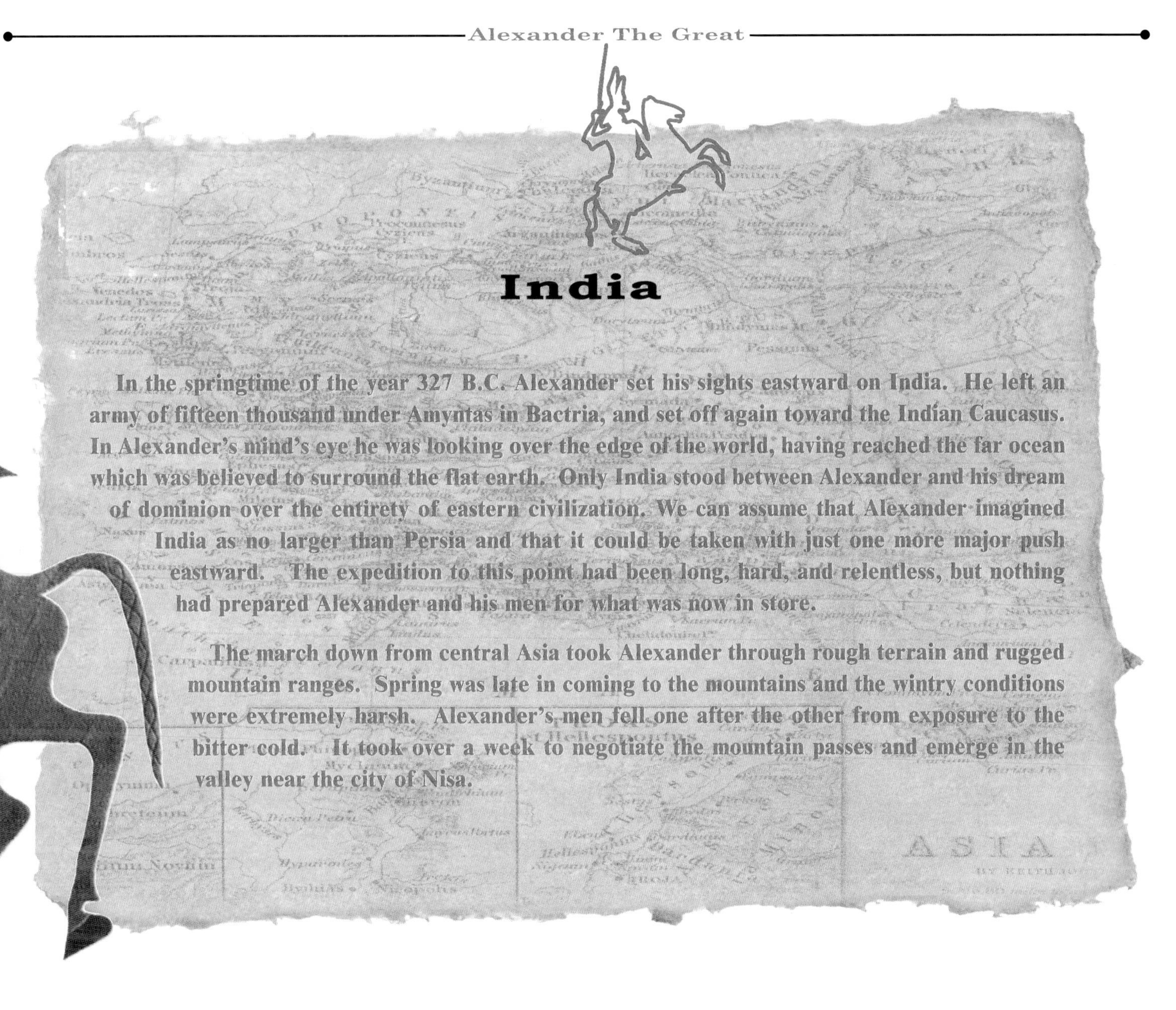

India

In the springtime of the year 327 B.C. Alexander set his sights eastward on India. He left an army of fifteen thousand under Amyntas in Bactria, and set off again toward the Indian Caucasus. In Alexander's mind's eye he was looking over the edge of the world, having reached the far ocean which was believed to surround the flat earth. Only India stood between Alexander and his dream of dominion over the entirety of eastern civilization. We can assume that Alexander imagined India as no larger than Persia and that it could be taken with just one more major push eastward. The expedition to this point had been long, hard, and relentless, but nothing had prepared Alexander and his men for what was now in store.

The march down from central Asia took Alexander through rough terrain and rugged mountain ranges. Spring was late in coming to the mountains and the wintry conditions were extremely harsh. Alexander's men fell one after the other from exposure to the bitter cold. It took over a week to negotiate the mountain passes and emerge in the valley near the city of Nisa.

The armies split into two parts, with Hephaestion and Perdiccas heading up one half and Alexander taking the other. Hephaestion's orders were to speed toward the Indus River, taking control of all settlements along the way. Alexander steered his force through the Aspasian territory along the River Choes, through rocky hills. They forged the river with difficulty, and sped off for the towns to the east, taking each one by fighting or agreement. As they neared the Aspasians, the natives ran off as soon as they became aware of Alexander's approach, escaping into the hills with the Macedonians on their heels. At the other side of the mountain range, Alexander took a settlement called Arigaeum, which had been deserted by its citizens and razed to the ground. He rejoined his troops with the other battalion, satisfied that his orders had been well carried out.

A large Indian force was camped on high ground near Arigaeum, and Ptolemy, who had gone ahead as a scout, reported to Alexander that the enemy had compiled a formidable army. When Alexander advanced toward them, the Indians, rather than maintain the advantage of their position on high, came down to meet them! The battle that ensued was bloody and the Indians fought courageously, but Alexander drove them off, keeping what he considered the finest prisoners to send back to Macedonia as slaves.

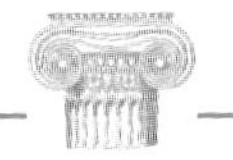

Alexander and the Wise Men

While in India, Alexander was often annoyed by reports that local sages and philosophers were preaching against him and his reign. These so-called Wise Men had even managed to stir up some minor revolts of the natives. After being wounded in battle with the Mallians and feeling sick and irritable during his recovery, Alexander had come to the end of his patience where the Indian sages were concerned.

A group of these had a habit of gathering in a meadow clearing, where they would sit and discuss philosophical matters. When Alexander came upon them by chance, he was surprised to observe that they did not rise in deference to the king. In fact they deigned to lecture him, reminding him of his mere mortality and declaring that he already possessed far more of the earth than the gods had ever meant to belong to a man.

Massaga, Bazira, and Ora all fell to Alexander after their defenses were broken. During the battles for these cities Alexander's men were introduced to beasts unlike any they had ever before encountered – elephants. The Macedonians marveled at their enormity, their strength, and their shining tusks which emerged like weapons from their mighty heads.

Throughout these campaigns the Indians had fought valiantly, but after the fall of Ora their nerve began to weaken and they began to see that their situation was without hope. Indians from throughout the district fled to the Rock of Aornos in hopes of finding refuge there. The "rock" is an enormous area of about twenty five miles around, and which stands at about eight thousand feet above the surface of the ground. Legend has it that Heracles tried but was unable to capture the mighty rock. Springs of pure water emerge from the highest portion of the rock, and forests and soil are plentiful enough to support a population of thousands.

Alexander was determined to capture the rock; all the more when he heard the story about Heracles' foiled attempt. He sent Hephaestion and Perdiccas toward the Indus, where they were to build a bridge and wait. Alexander began to march a portion of the armies toward the Aornos. His plan was to cut off supplies to the Rock and break the Indians by means of siege. This did not turn out to be necessary, however, since within one day of fighting, the Indians were overpowered

Alexander arrested the impertinent philosophers and appointed a judge to decide their fate. By way of a trial, Alexander stood before the men, asking them questions to which he anyway wished to have answers. It was agreed that if the judge deemed the answers to be unworthy, the Wise Men would be executed.

Alexander approached the first philosopher and asked him: "Of which are there a greater number, living men, or dead?" The reply came, "The living, since the dead are no long men."

The second philosopher received the question: "Which contains more creatures, the sea or the earth?" The wise man did not hesitate to come back with, "the earth, as the sea is but part of the earth!"

Alexander was greatly pleased with these answers but endeavored to appear noncommittal in front of the judge, who supposedly had the final word. He moved on to the next

and withdrew. Alexander offered sacrifices to the gods in thanks for his ability to occupy the Rock which had eluded Heracles.

Coming down from Aornos, Alexander pressed on into the Assacenian territory, and onward to the Indus. As they passed the city of Nisa, the town chief came out to greet Alexander, prostrating himself on the ground until Alexander asked him to get up and state his business. The chief then begged Alexander to preserve his city's freedom, in honor of the god Dionysus, who according to legend had founded Nisa and populated it with his priests. The nearby mountain peak was called Merus, which meant "thigh" in commemoration of Dionysus' being born from the thigh of Zeus. The chief explained that Nisa had always been free and independent, existing according to its own laws and statutes.

philosopher. "Which came first, the day or the night?" To this he received the answer, "The day, by a day." Alexander was not sure what to make of this answer, and after contemplation he simply responded, "Strange questions sometimes produce strange answers…."

Alexander's next query was: "How can a man make himself loved?"
The philosopher looked into the king's eyes and answered, "He must be very powerful, but never too much feared". Alexander nodded knowingly at this answer, and lingered in front of this philosopher for a brief moment.

Alexander's last three queries were issues of utmost importance which had occupied him for some a good portion of his life. "How can a man become a god?" he shot at one of the Wise ones. The philosopher who fielded this question was brave enough to answer, "A man can never become a god", he said, "It is impossible."

Furthermore, ivy, the plant of the gods, grew thickly in the area – the only place in India where ivy had taken root.

Alexander was greatly pleased to hear that he had already penetrated as far into India as had Dionysus. Sacrifices were offered, and the Macedonians delighted in the abundant ivy which they had not seen since leaving home. They fashioned wreaths and bracelets from the leaves and stems and prayed to Dionysus with thanks. Alexander agreed that Nisa should continue as an autonomous political entity, and asked its citizens to provide him with reinforcements of cavalry and other troops.

"Which is stronger? Life or death?" was Alexander's subsequent question.

The answer: "Life. Life endures far more than does death."

Alexander had one remaining question. It surprised those assembled at the trial. Choosing one of the Wise Men, Alexander approached him with the challenge, "How long must a man live?"

To this question the philosopher could find no answer. He remained silent for a time, and when finally his response came, it was evasive and vague. Alexander was disappointed, but not angry.

The questions and answers were considered and weighed, and the judge was asked for his verdict. "Death to the Wise Men", was his decree, and the assemblage concurred. Alexander, however, did not. He had been greatly impressed with the responses to his queries as well as by the philosophers' courage and wit. All were set free.

Dissatisfaction in the Ranks

Throughout this first period of the Indian campaign, rumblings of dissatisfaction and disillusionment became louder and more insistent among Alexander's men. Alexander had taken more and more to eastern ways, and had ceased wearing Macedonian garb even when in the presence of his own closest companions. Now even the long-serving Macedonians who had been his friends from the first were required to kneel and prostrate themselves when coming into the royal presence. This did not sit well with some of the veterans in Alexander's closest assemblage. Resentments ran high, and although most obeyed the new commands, they did so under silent protest. Callisthenes, a nephew of Aristotle who had been with the expedition since the beginning as its official historian, was one of the most respected members of Alexander's entourage. He had seen all of the changes the young King had undergone, and experienced first hand all of the high and low points of the adventure. He was loyal to his King, but his stronger loyalty was to his own principles. He simply would not kneel on the ground or lay prostrate before any man! At an official banquet where Alexander passed a loving cup around the table, he passed it first to those who had agreed to prostration. As each man kneeled and lay on the ground, then drank, he

received a kiss from Alexander. Callisthenes, however, simply took a sip from the cup, and presented himself to be kissed. Alexander refused to kiss him, and Callisthenes simply announced, "Well, I shall be one kiss the poorer then". Callisthenes went on to make an impassioned speech to the assembled company. He declared the Alexander was deserving of the highest honors paid to men, but that it should be forbidden to worship a man as one would a god. He expounded on the dangers of treating a man as a deity, reminding Alexander that not even Heracles was afforded divine honors. He described the differences in practice between honoring a man and a god. Gods, he pointed out, have temples dedicated to them, hymns composed for them, and sacrifices made to them. Men greet one another with physical contact such as a kiss, while it is forbidden to touch the gods.

Therefore one must bow down and touch the earth in their presence. Furthermore, he added, to pay too much homage to a man is to denigrate the gods by attempting to raise mortals to their level.

The Macedonians who heard this dissertation heartily agreed with its logic and sentiment, and Alexander was forced in the name of keeping the peace among the ranks to rescind the order for them to prostrate themselves before him in the future. He was, however, greatly disturbed and angry at what he thought of as Callisthenes' disloyalty. Chances are that Alexander had never really liked Callisthenes, and despite Alexander's own growing arrogance, the historian was himself out of place with his rude behavior toward the King.

Soon after these events unfolded, a plot to assassinate Alexander was revealed. The plot was foiled when one of Alexander's trusted seers suggested he spend the night out drinking rather than in his bed, and the murderers didn't find their prey. The conspiracy was carried out by a group of young sons of Macedonian nobles who resented Alexander for embarrassing one of them, when the boy had most likely saved his life. The boys, when interrogated, claimed that Callisthenes had put them up to the crime. Alexander was not surprised and readily believed in Callisthenes culpability. Callisthenes met a cruel fate at the hands of the angry young king. He was dragged along with the army in chains, tortured and abused, until his health gave out. There are conflicting reports as to Callisthenes' final demise, some saying he was hanged, and others that he simply passed away from illness.

Onward and Eastward

Hephaestion had meanwhile completed construction of the bridge over the Indus, and Alexander brought the rest of the army to meet him. They camped on the banks of the river for the remainder of the winter, and when spring came, they crossed over uneventfully. Taxiles, the Indian ruler of a territory called Taxila, in the area between the Indus and Hydaspes River, was summoned to a meeting with Alexander and he arrived in friendship and welcoming, bearing valuable gifts, including twenty five elephants, oxen, and sheep, in addition to hundreds of silver talents. Taxiles had no intention of fighting the Macedonians, and faced Alexander without fear, saying "why should we fight? I will share my riches with you and I will not scorn riches you offer me in return." This attitude won Alexander's immediate respect, and the two men formed an alliance. Alexander halted his expedition long enough to hold athletic contests and to make sacrifices again.

When his seers declared the time was auspicious for the next river crossing, he again got on the move.

The Last Great Battle

The troops pressed on toward the Hydaspes, a wide river which cut through the territory later called Punjab, in northwestern India. The area was ruled by a mighty king called Porus who had already taken hold of the eastern bank of the Hydaspes with a great force of men. Porus was determined to stop Alexander short at the river either by thwarting the Macedonians' attempt to cross it, or by overwhelming them on the other side. Alexander took his time and patiently carved out a strategy for outwitting Porus and getting his men over in good form for attack. He ordered all the boats which had been used for the Indus crossing be brought forward and cut into smaller vessels. He divided his forces into several contingents and spread them out along the river bank in order to keep Porus guessing as to where the Macedonians might be planning to come across. Then he kept these detachments on the move, changing their positions frequently. The men took to whooping and hollering loudly at intervals as if they were any moment about to make off swiftly for the other side. After many of these "false alarms", Porus and his officers tired of the game and began to think that Alexander's men were never really going to budge. They allowed their watch to become lax, giving Alexander a perfect edge. At a point where the river was divided by a large peninsula jutting out from the opposite shore, he waited until a stormy night to make his move.

Under cover of darkness, clamorous thunderclaps and driving rain, Alexander moved his troops across the river in boats and using the cloth and straw floats. Only when they made the opposite bank did they realize their mistake; the "peninsula" was actually an island! There still remained another crossing before they would attain their enemy's territory! It was almost dawn by the time the troops managed to cross clear to the opposite bank. It had been a treacherous endeavor, and the men and horses were at the limit of their endurance, but they had eluded the enemy and made it ashore intact.

Alexander was the first to disembark and assess the situation. He was brought word that Porus' forces were massed not far from their point of landing, and that Porus' son was heading toward them with an elite army. Alexander arranged his men into fighting formation as quickly as he could and set out to face the enemy on the offensive. When the Indians caught sight of Alexander approaching with his cavalry, they broke rank and fled. Porus' son was one of the first killed among heavy Indian casualties.

Indian messengers hastily reported to Porus what had happened, including the death of his son, and that the Macedonians had succeeded in landing all of their troops and equipment intact. Porus decided to face Alexander himself, and he started toward the Macedonian position with a force of four thousand cavalry, three hundred chariots, and hundreds of elephants. The rest of his army, which numbered almost thirty thousand in all, was made up of his best infantry units.

The recent rains had rendered the earth muddy and slippery, making advancement difficult for the men, horses, and chariots. Alexander had halted his men, and they waited as the enemy slogged slowly toward them. When the Indians came within range, Alexander attacked fiercely, sending mounted archers around the Indians' left flank, and following immediately with a cavalry attack by the King's Companions. When the Indians seemed to reel in confusion, Alexander attacked again, splitting the Indian force into two. Alexander drove down the middle of the enemy's formation, toppled the elephant drivers, and poured missiles onto the Indian troops. The phalanx advanced toward the elephants, and the infantry behind them began to retreat. Alexander sent units in all direction, ordering them to encircle the enemy. The elephants themselves began to tire, and they lumbered backward, their trumpeting becoming feebler. The Indian cavalry was all but massacred, the survivors turning and fleeing through a gap in the Macedonian noose hold. The Indians suffered heavy losses, numbering at least twenty-three thousand. Their war chariots were destroyed, and most of their horses and elephants fell captive. Porus lost two of his sons in this battle. The Macedonians sustained a loss of eighty infantry and two hundred cavalry.

Porus handled himself throughout this debacle with the nobility and courage which befit a king. Unlike the hapless Darius, Porus did not turn and flee to save his own skin when the battle turned and all was lost. Covered almost completely in armor, he fought on bravely amongst his dead soldiers, and did not withdraw until he himself sustained a serious wound to his right shoulder, virtually the only part of his body which was unprotected. Porus retreated on elephant-back with his entourage.

Alexander was greatly moved by Porus' behavior, and tried several times to send him a message offering friendship and respect. The first ambassador to approach Porus was Taxiles. When Taxiles rode up to Porus announcing Alexander's desire to make contact, Porus turned on his elephant and tried to spear him with his lance. Taxiles narrowly escaped with his life. Alexander kept trying until at last Meroes, an Indian who had been Porus' friend, was received by Porus and heard Alexander's message. Porus asked to be taken to the Macedonian.

Alexander and a group of his Companions rode toward the Indian king and greeted him with ceremony. Porus was an imposing figure – at least seven feet in height, extremely handsome and of proud bearing. He faced Alexander with all of his pride intact, exuding the air of a king, not of the vanquished. Alexander, after the appropriate greetings, asked the Indian: "What would you ask of me?" Porus replied, "Treat me as a King". Alexander answered that in any case he would certainly do this, and gave him another chance at a request, saying, "Is there nothing more you would like?" Porus answered, "Everything of importance is covered in what I have asked".

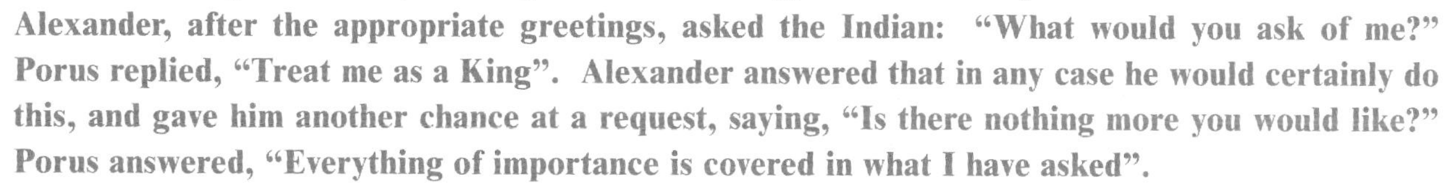

Alexander was impressed with Porus' bravery in battle and pleased by the dignity he displayed in this exchange. He granted the Indian king continued sovereignty over his subjects and even added to his realm. The two formed a fast friendship and were loyal to one another to the end. Alexander founded a city near the Hydaspes; Nicaea, near the spot where his armies had crossed the river.

There were still more battles in India, to be sure, but none were of consequence and they were easily won. The battle against Porus at the Hydaspes was the last great contest of Alexander the Great's armies on the great adventure. It was now the summer of 326 B.C.

Bucephalus Heralds the End

It is said that animals possess an uncanny knowledge and intuition that humans cannot access. Perhaps Bucephalus sensed that the end was near, and wished to demonstrate that to his beloved master. Or perhaps, being very old and having wearied of the march, it was simply his time. At any rate, Bucephalus died soon after the battle against Porus. He may have been wounded during the conflict but this is unlikely, since Alexander had long since taken to riding younger and swifter animals in battle, and kept Bucephalus at a safe distance from danger. More likely, the great steed had simply come to the end of his endurance and passed away peacefully.

Alexander mourned the noble creature as intensely as if he had been human. After completing the funeral rights for his fallen soldiers, and offering the usual sacrifices to the gods for the victory, Alexander saw to the burial of Bucephalus, and grieved desolately for his friend. It was around this time that Alexander's trusty dog Peritas passed away as well. Peritas had been a loyal and adored companion. Alexander founded two additional cities in India and named them for his beloved animals. Losing both creatures in such a short span of time was very painful for Alexander, but he did not take heed of the deaths as a prophecy of the end of the expedition, as perhaps he should have...

Alexander and his armies regrouped after the great battle, and continued their trek into the deep interior of India. They came upon numerous small kingdoms and villages – and took each one with a minimum of difficulty. The landscape was unchanging, dusty, and dry. Alexander's objective was the Granges River, which he believed fed into the Outer Ocean surrounding the earth. He planned to subdue the Indian tribes that populated the riversides, and to follow it to its mouth. After continuing for only one hundred miles, however, the Macedonian army refused to continue on.

The Politest of Mutinies.

If Alexander took stock of his situation at that time, he would have counted eleven thousand miles over which he and his men had traveled in the span of eight years. Many of the troops were the original men who set out with their beloved king and had not been home since. The vision and the charisma of their leader had carried them all the way into India – an almost unimaginable distance from their native Greece and Macedonia. They had shared the vision, and understood its purpose. Their morale had been high and their resolute desire which matched Alexander's was a burning motivation. These carried them across the Hellespont, along the Mediterranean and all the way to Egypt, then to Persia. They had followed their king willingly and proudly almost the entire length of the known world. Whenever lapses of will to continue had occurred, and they had in the last couple of years especially, Alexander had been able to successfully counter them and convince his men to continue the adventure and to follow him yet further toward the "end of the earth".

Now, however, it seemed that Alexander's armies had truly lost a vital element making up their collective will. The expedition seemed never ending and a sense of futility set in. The very vastness of India perhaps put them off and made them feel their exhaustion acutely. The "end of the earth" still seemed too far off, and the men longed to see home again. They hankered to be welcomed as heroes while they still had the strength to enjoy their achievements, and they wanted to reunite with their families. All of these sentiments had certainly been with the men all along, but now these came to the fore as their dominant drives. The continuation of the adventure had lost its luster and purpose. "Enough" was the overwhelming response to the thought of the next push onward.

Alexander tried his usual tactics to re-motivate his men, including childish moping along with impassioned orations. He declared that any man that followed him would not be sorry! He paraded naked in front of the troops pointing out his own wounds and scars from battle. He promised that those who remained with him would enjoy the most exalted glory, and be showered with spoils and riches. This time, however, nothing worked. Though Alexander's words moved his men deeply, they refused to march on. While their king lay in his tent waiting to hear that the troops had reconsidered and they would push forward after all, the men milled around outside, patiently waiting for their king to accept the inevitable and announce that it was time to return home. Love for Alexander was still the dominant sentiment. The men were sorry to cause their leader to be despondent, and yet they remained resolute in their refusal to move another step into the reaches of India. The Great Adventure was over. It was time to turn back. Alexander had said many times that he would never hold a soldier in his army against his will, and that all were free to leave whenever they might. Now that the majority wanted to end the expedition, Alexander would have no choice but to comply, heartbroken though he may be.

After three days of isolation and soul searching, Alexander emerged and announced that he would bow to the wishes of his loyal troops. It was time to turn around – not in retreat, but to return.

The Long March Home

Alexander rallied himself and put his deep disappointment aside, as he made ready to lead his troops on the long march for home. He convinced his closest companions that the route home would begin after they had seen the Indian Ocean. This meant a river trip down the Hydaspes and the Indus, after which they would indeed turn westward. Alexander may have believed that the Indus and Nile rivers were one and the same, and therefore he saw this as a chance to reach the mouth of the Nile. Before they set off, Alexander ordered his artisans to fashion larger than life versions of armor, weapons, and equipment, which he had scattered throughout the area for posterity. He wished future generations that would come across these objects to marvel at the greatness of the Macedonian warriors!

Back at the Hydaspes they paused for a time to increase their fleet of boats and rafts. When all was ready, the departure was marked by a solemn and celebratory ceremony complete with trumpets blaring and prayers tot he gods for a successful journey. Alexander and his closest entourage, along with part of his armies sailed on the water while the rest of the men marched along both sides of the river on the banks. The journey down the river began in November, 326 B.C. As the armies made their way downstream, they encountered communities situated on the river. For the most part, these villages would not surrender without fighting, but the Macedonians subdued them easily, and replenished their supply stores at each settlement. When they reached the Indus, they continued southward with in the same manner, the forces split between the watercraft and the overland trek.

As they approached the territory of the Mallians the mood easy trip became more dangerous. Alexander had already heard that the Malli villagers were the most aggressive of the Indian peoples and that their warriors were fierce and courageous. The Mallians had fortified their largest towns and shut their women, children and infirm inside the walls. Their intentions to stand firm against the Macedonians were obvious, and Alexander prepared for a fight. Their largest city was indeed a mighty fortress, with high walls impossible to scale without ladders. Alexander ordered ladders be fashioned quickly, and he was the first to climb to the top and peer into the city. From his perch on top, he acted quickly, dropping into the town and surprising the local watchmen, who thought they had seen a ghost and fled. When they looked back, however, they regained their courage when they saw Alexander was still alone, and they rushed back to attack him. As they gained on him, Alexander was joined by several of his own soldiers and they scuffled with the Mallians, killing them. In the struggle, however, Alexander was gravely injured by an arrow which pierced his breastplate and entered his rib cage. In addition, he was stabbed in the neck with a sword. The Macedonians managed to carry Alexander over the wall and back to safety. Meanwhile, the rest of the forces, incensed and grieved at the news that their king had been hurt, overran the town and subdued the Mallians. Alexander's would was quite serious, and removal of the arrowhead dangerous and painful. He recovered slowly, and during his recuperation he received the overwhelming support of his men. Rumors circulated in the camp that Alexander had died, and the men were beside themselves with remorse at the way they had cut short his

dream, and grateful that he had allowed them to do so. The mood was so desperate that Alexander dragged himself from his sickbed, donned a nightshirt, and appeared at the door of his tent to prove that he was still alive. The troops cheered and wept with joy when Alexander regained his strength and announced it was time to move on downriver.

In July 325 B.C. after a seven month voyage, Alexander and his fleet met his armies at the mouth of the Indus River, where it fed into the Indian Ocean. Alexander was overjoyed to have come this far; he sacrificed to the gods, praying that no future conqueror should surpass his achievements.

Westward

Alexander was now ready to leave India behind. Dividing his forces again, he sent a fleet of boats under the command of Nearchus out to the Indian Ocean, sailing westward in the Persian Gulf. Leading the rest of his men himself, he set out overland across the desolate Mekran desert along the coast. For weeks he and his troops plied the harsh, punishing westward trail. They suffered from thirst, exhaustion, hunger, and heat, and many died along the way. Almost all of the animals perished in the burning hot sand. They marched day and night to escape their predicament with all possible speed. When scouts did discover water, Alexander would halt his men a good mile from its source to prevent them from flinging themselves upon it desperately, spoiling its purity and making themselves sick from drinking too much too quickly. These turned out to be the most punishing conditions the Macedonians had encountered in all their nine years of war.

After several weeks, Alexander and his surviving troops reached a fertile strip called Gedrosia where they were able to rest. The natives there greeted the armies with open arms and provided them with water and nourishment. Alexander collapsed with relief, and perhaps had what could be called a mild nervous breakdown after nearly perishing during the dessert ordeal. He allowed his men to run amok, and he himself drank and feasted without pause for a week.

Rallying himself and the men, Alexander pushed on, founding and naming cities in his wake, on his way back to Persia by way of Carmania. Alexander's return to Persia came not a moment too soon, as things were in disarray due to the long absence of the ruler. Many of the governors

Alexander had appointed had assumed long since that he was dead or at least would never return, and these officials began taking advantage of their people, causing dissatisfaction and unrest among the Persian populous. Alexander had his work cut out for him, and he marched from province to province, town to town, routing out the corrupt officers and replacing them, trying to restore order and confidence. In 324 B.C. Alexander and his armies returned to Persepolis. Alexander was thirty two years of age. The journey from India had taken eighteen months.

Word coming back from Greece and Macedonia was disheartening. It seemed that Olympias and her daughters had attempted to overthrow Antipater, and tried to divide Macedonia between them! Numerous letters were exchanged between Alexander and his mother, and between the King and Antipater, as he tried to mediate between them. Antipater complained that the Queen was headstrong and temperamental, and that she insisted on meddling in affairs which were not hers to control. Olympias, for her part tried to lower Alexander's estimation of Antipater by calling him arrogant and claiming that he was demanding a kinglike respect from their compatriots.

Meanwhile, Alexander's sea admiral, Nearchus, had managed to land the fleet and forge his way inland with a few soldiers. When he caught up with Alexander Nearchus was in such a bad physical state that Alexander barely recognized him. When he did, he embraced the seaman, thinking he had lost the entire fleet, and began to weep. When Nearchus reassured Alexander that the fleet was safe, Alexander wept again, this time from joy and celebration.

Alexander had long planned to search out the tomb of Cyrus the Great, the founder of the Persian Empire. At this juncture, Alexander was finally led to the tomb, but to his surprise and consternation, he found it had long since been destroyed and looted. The remains of Cyrus had been taken, and his golden coffin damaged when the thieves attempted to break it into pieces and reduce its enormous weight for removal. The inscription on the tomb was still legible, and it read: "Oh Man, whosoever you may be, I am Cyrus the son of Cambyses, founder of the Empire of Persia, and ruler of Asia. Do not grudge me my monument nor the bit of earth that covers my bones."

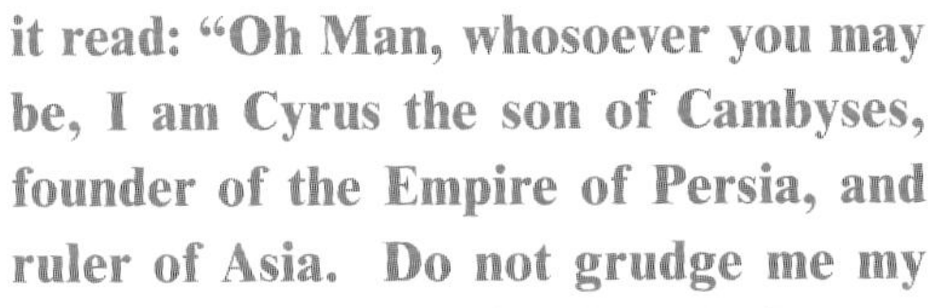

Alexander ordered that the monument and the tomb be completely restored and that replicas of all its reported contents be supplied. He arrested the apparently incompetent guards and had them tortured, hoping they would reveal the identity of the culprits. They did not, and after a time Alexander released them. The new tomb was sealed with stone and covered with plaster, in which was set the image of the royal seal.

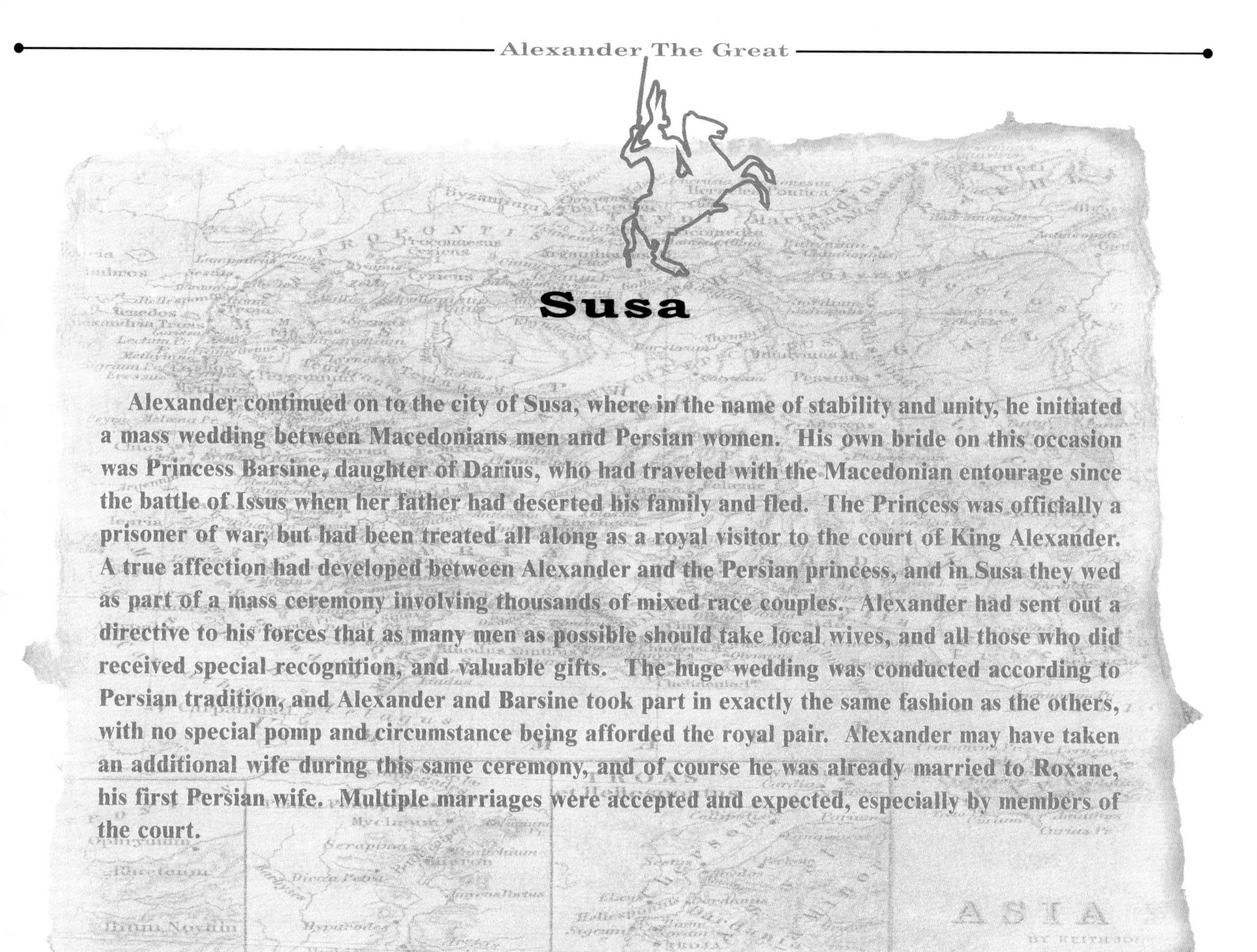

Susa

Alexander continued on to the city of Susa, where in the name of stability and unity, he initiated a mass wedding between Macedonians men and Persian women. His own bride on this occasion was Princess Barsine, daughter of Darius, who had traveled with the Macedonian entourage since the battle of Issus when her father had deserted his family and fled. The Princess was officially a prisoner of war, but had been treated all along as a royal visitor to the court of King Alexander. A true affection had developed between Alexander and the Persian princess, and in Susa they wed as part of a mass ceremony involving thousands of mixed race couples. Alexander had sent out a directive to his forces that as many men as possible should take local wives, and all those who did received special recognition, and valuable gifts. The huge wedding was conducted according to Persian tradition, and Alexander and Barsine took part in exactly the same fashion as the others, with no special pomp and circumstance being afforded the royal pair. Alexander may have taken an additional wife during this same ceremony, and of course he was already married to Roxane, his first Persian wife. Multiple marriages were accepted and expected, especially by members of the court.

Hephaestion also married a princess, the youngest daughter of Darius, Drypetis, who was chosen for him by Alexander. Alexander was enchanted with the idea that his dearest friend was not his brother-in-law and that they would be uncles to one another's children. Craterus married Amastrin, Darius' nephew, and Perdiccas was wed to a daughter of the governor of Media. Ptolemy and several other generals were also betrothed to daughters of prominent Persian officials.

The marriage feast was magnificent and lavish. Alexander gifted each groom with a gold cup, and forgave all debts of the newlywed men. He also gave cash awards for good service and bravery. At the end of the evening over ten thousand Macedonian soldiers took their Persian brides back to their quarters. It had truly been a "marriage of East and West".

Marriage to Persian women did nothing to rekindle the spirit of the Macedonian armies however. Where once there had been hardness and precision, now there was softness and staleness. Alexander himself took more and more to drink and evil habits, and much of his fresh charm and vitality seemed to seep from his person, leaving only a shell of his former self.

Around the time of the mass wedding, an occurrence of horrible significance tore at Alexander's peace of mind. Calanus, an elderly Indian seer, traveled with the Macedonians and was a dear friend to the young king. Calanus seemed to lately be sensing that nothing good was afoot and that an unfortunate end was near. While in India, Calanus had never suffered a single day of illness. Since arriving in Persia however, his strength had failed him and he had become quite feeble. He would take no treatment, saying he was ready to die, since at any rate things were about to turn quite dire. Alexander begged him to try to regain his health, but he was obstinate in his refusal. Calanus begged Alexander to have a funeral pyre built for him, and after much protestation, Alexander finally agreed to his request. Calanus, who was too weak to walk, was carried to the pyre amid solemn ceremony, singing Indian hymns, and dressed in rich robes and garlands. After taking his leave of all those who were dear to him, Calanus climbed onto the pyre, lay down upon it, and attendants lit the fire. Alexander and the assembled company were astonished that Calanus made not one flinching movement as the flames engulfed him. He did not moan or cry out, nor shrink in any way from the fire. Alexander was deeply moved by this spectacle, and immediately afterward called for Hephaestion to join him in a night of drinking. The two became drunk, and Alexander cried out that he would award a solid gold crown to whichever man would consume the most drink. The man who won the crown that night died three days later of alcohol poisoning, followed by forty one other men who had competed with him for the prize. Alexander wept, as he seemed to be doing often during this period, and mourned the men who had drunken themselves to death at his behest.

Alexander's Great Speech

A special group of thirty thousand Asian boys had been undergoing training with the Macedonians, and around this time they received their ranks and joined Alexander's force. Alexander had considered this an experiment to see if the easterners could indeed match muster with the Macedonians, and the trial was declared a resounding success. Alexander was pleased with the discipline, robustness, and talent of the Asian soldiers. He chose from among their number his new personal bodyguard, made up of a small group of hand-picked men. His guard was now, for the first time, not only inclusive of Persian members, but exclusively Persian. The veteran Macedonians were incensed and hurt by this and protested vehemently. They demonstrated outside his tent for three days until Alexander finally emerged and again, wept. He thanked the men for their loyalty and said that they would always be bound to him as kin, but the Persian bodyguard remained in service, and resentment continued to smolder in the Macedonian ranks.

Alexander got his forces on the move again, ordering Hephaestion to go down to the Persian Gulf with half the infantry and camp there. Alexander and the rest of the armies boarded the fleet which was waiting near Susa, and sailed down the Eulaeus River to the sea. There he continued on in the Gulf with only his Companions, to the mouth of the Tigris, leaving the rest of the fleet to sail back up to the canal which they passed through to the Tigris. Sailing up the Tigris, they met Hephaestion and the rest of the troops. They continued on to a town called Opis, and there they stopped to rest and to take care of administrative matters.

Alexander had decided to send home a number of his troops who were no longer fit for service by reason of age or infirmity, and he called an assembly to announce this intention. He promised that each one would be honorably discharged and were to receive gifts that would make them the envy of their friends and relatives. Alexander likely believed the men would be grateful for such consideration, but their reaction was quite the opposite. Not only did the discharged soldiers themselves feel insulted at being dismissed, but the entire army seemed to rise up in emotional outburst, crying out to Alexander again about his adoption of Persian dress and behavior, his inclusion of foreigners in the elite fighting units, and his insistence that his father was the god Ammon, and not the mortal Philip.

Alexander was absolutely incensed at this outburst. His first impulsive reaction was to execute thirteen of the leaders of this demonstration. He had become considerably less patient of late and quicker to anger, and discharged his violent energy first, and used words later. Following the deaths of the ring leaders, Alexander delivered a long impromptu speech from a special dais facing thousands of his men. With all of the pent up frustration and emotion in his being, he addressed the armies passionately and eloquently.

Alexander cataloged all that his father Philip had done for the Macedonians, followed by his own military history, and the pride he had heaped upon his followers. He listed his military victories, pointing out that each one had been in the name of them, his countrymen. He described the dangerous battles and the valorous deeds of his leaders and his common soldiers. Alexander truthfully mentioned his own unselfishness and his comradely behavior with his troops, taking nothing more for his personal comfort than he would give to any one of his men. His unselfishness, his fairness, and his integrity were noted.

Alexander reminded his men that he had forgiven their debts, paid them handsomely at every step of the journey, and afforded them every comfort and luxury available during the grand adventure. He recounted his treatment of the dead, and of their families back in Greece and Macedonia. He retold of his care for the wounded, and for the mates and children of the troops.

The king finished his speech with a dismissal of all who would still take their leave of him in good conscience. “Go then!” he shouted. “Get out of my sight!”

Alexander jumped from the rostrum and disappeared into his tent. For two days he would not take food, did not wash, and did not allow anyone to visit him. When finally he did communicate,

it was to his Persian guard whom he called "kinsmen", and they gave him the customary kiss.

During his confinement, the Macedonians stood silently around Alexander's tent. When they realized he was stirring, they started lamenting their selfish behavior and begging his forgiveness. Hearing this, Alexander emerged. He was about to address them, but before he spoke, his elder officer Callines, of the King's Companions, cried out that the Macedonians were insulted yet again since the Persian "kinsmen" had been allowed to kiss the king when no Macedonian had been allowed within range! Alexander replied that all of the Macedonians were truly his kinsmen and would be called so from that moment forward. Callines kissed the King, followed by all the Macedonians who were so inclined.

Alexander, grateful that harmony seemed to be restored, offered sacrifices to the gods and held a banquet for nine thousand men at which he seated himself among the Macedonians, behind whom he seated the Persians. The unfit and older soldiers were indeed discharged and went home with enough pay to last the journey, plus a generous cash gift. The veterans were given a warm send-off by Alexander who sincerely thanked them for their distinguished service. Those who had fathered Asian children were asked to leave them behind, and Alexander promised to look after their education himself, and to return them fully grown and educated to Macedonia! The crowd was dissolved in tears by the time the good-byes had all been said.

Craterus was charged with seeing the departing troops home, and once there he was to take over the administration of Macedonia from Antipater. Alexander had apparently tired of his mother's constant complaints about the old general, or perhaps he'd truly been influenced by her comments and requests, and finally bowed to her wishes to have Antipater replaced.

More Tragedy

After the great feast of thanksgiving Alexander must have felt sure that the worst was behind him. The armies started off again, united behind their leader, toward the Kingdom of Medes. On their arrival in the city of Ecbatana, Alexander offered his customary sacrifices of celebration and gratitude, and quickly organized a festive round of sporting contests for the men to enjoy. As had become his habit of late, he spent most of his evenings drinking with his cronies. During this period of relative calm, Hephaestion began to feel unwell. Though he suffered from a fever, he allowed himself to be persuaded to join Alexander in a drinking party, soon after which his illness became quite serious. On the seventh day of Hephaestion's suffering, Alexander was overseeing a footrace at the stadium, when an urgent message was delivered informing the king that the general's conditioned had taken a turn for the worse. Alexander rushed to Hephaestion's side, but by the time he arrived at the sickbed, it was too late. His lifelong friend was dead. Alexander's relationship with Hephaestion was the closest and most enduring of his life. His friend meant more to him than any man or woman, and his death was almost more than he could bear. Alexander's anguish at losing Hephaestion far surpassed all mourning he had experienced in the past, and by some accounts he went quite literally mad with grief. He cast himself over the body of his friend and refused to be moved for over a day. He lay weeping on Hephaestion's corpse and shouted out vicious accusations at whoever was brave enough to enter the tent. Alexander's fiercest anger was directed at the physician who had been unable to save his cherished companion, and at various others who had witnessed Hephaestion's drinking and not forced him to stop.

For two full days Alexander took no nourishment, did not bathe, and cried inconsolably. When he emerged from Hephaestion's tent he had his hair chopped off as a sign of bereavement, and ordered the construction of an elaborate funeral pyre. An official period of mourning was declared throughout the kingdom. Funeral games were held, with thousands participating in contests of every kind. By the end of the games Alexander seemed to emerge somewhat from his overwhelming sorrow. He announced that no replacement would be named for the command of the King's Companions cavalry unit. They would forever be called "Hephaestion's Regiment" and carry his image into every battle.

Alexander as a diver.

Never the Same

Alexander never recovered fully from the loss of Hephaestion. His personality and behavior continued to deteriorate, and his delusions of grandeur became more and more pronounced. He considered a suggestion to have his likeness carved out of a huge living mountain, such that it would be seen for hundreds of miles. According to the artists plan, Alexander's hand alone would be large enough to house a city of ten thousand souls. The plan was rejected; Alexander considered it not grand enough a tribute to such as himself!

Perhaps to drown his misery and to distract himself from his suffering, he declared war against the Cossaeans, a weak mountain people in the area of the Uxians. Alexander pounced upon them with unusual and unnecessary savagery, destroying them completely.

Back to Babylon

Alexander sent his fleet ahead under the command of Nearchus, and he set off with his armies toward Babylon. Before they reached the city, they were met by a party of Chaldaean Wise Men who warned Alexander that disaster would surely strike him if he should enter Babylon. They begged the King to curtain his march and stay clear of the danger by turning eastward from where they now were. They evoked the name of their god Bel, who had supposedly foretold that entering the city would be fatal for Alexander. Although always in the past he had been respectful of the prophecies of seers and diviners, now Alexander ignored the warnings and kept marching westward. He entertained a certain suspicion that the Chaldaeans had reason to want to keep him out of Babylon and had fabricated the signs. Perhaps they disapproved of his plan to raze their Temple of Bel in order to build a new shrine.

When the walls of Babylon came into sight, an ominous sign was observed. A huge flock of crows blackened the sky, cawing loudly and fighting with one another. Alexander's seers interpreted this as an omen portending the worst possible disaster. If this were not enough – when Alexander slaughtered a beast for sacrifice, observers reported that the animal had a deformed liver. Alexander was informed by his soothsayers that this too was an extremely grave warning, and they too warned against entering the city.

Alexander set up his quarters on a houseboat near Babylon. From there he went into town infrequently and always highly protected by his personal guards. He grew restless and fearful, almost paranoid, and often went into tirades of remorse over deeds he had committed in the past. He had wide mood swings and hysterical outbursts, and became increasingly uneasy and unhappy.

Alexander sent a party of envoys to the shrine of Ammon and impatiently awaited their answer. The envoys queried Ammon as to the status of the dead Hephaestion. Alexander wished to know with what honors his dead friend could be bestowed. The answer came that Alexander would be permitted to offer sacrifices to Hephaestion as to a "demi-god". This answer pleased Alexander greatly, and he proceeded to honor Hephaestion daily with a hero's sacrifice. He ordered the construction of a number of shrines to his companion in several of the cities in his empire, including Alexandria Egypt, and on the island of Pharos.

When one of the king's oracles assisted him in communicating with Hephaestion, Alexander was so excited and pleased by this event that he called for a great banquet to be held in celebration. At this feast he began to drink during the meal, and continued drinking until well into the following day. When he finally rested, upon rising he felt a sharp pain between his shoulders. The pain did not subside, and was soon accompanied by a high fever as well. His strength ebbed quickly, and he was able to do no more than bath, and eat a little each day for several days. From his sick bed he passed on orders to his officers who carried out his wishes and administered his business. He ordered his men to be ready in a few days to continue their march. The fever never broke. Alexander ceased rising to bathe and eat, and simply lay on his couch, conscious but unmoving.

After Alexander

When Alexander lay dying from his final illness, it seems that even his closest friends and companions labored under the belief that he was indeed invincible and would rise again from this affliction as he had from every wound and illness he had suffered in the past. Little effort was taken to extract from the great leader the appointment of a successor! There were no reported bedside conferences and no "last words" offered as instructions to him who would inherit the vastness that was Alexander's.

The only report of any discussion of the matter during the final days of Alexander's life states that when queried as to who should lead in his place, the dying king answered "The Strongest". This was a vague directive indeed, and served little to assist the various generals to whom it fell to administer such a vast estate.

The years after Alexander's death were marked by chaos and strife, as

The End

On June 1, 323 B.C. Alexander's attendants carried him outside to a shady park hoping the fresh air would revive him. On June 2 they brought him back inside. Alexander woke up long enough to direct his caretakers not to allow entrance into his presence to anyone they did not trust. On the 7th, Alexander's fever rose further still, and he lapsed into a coma. Many thought the king was already dead, and they filed passed his bed, paying respects. A long line of Macedonians silently crept by, as the King still clung to life.

On June 10, 323 B.C. Alexander the Great died. He was thirty-three years old. He was intensely mourned by the Macedonian forces and by people all across the great empire.

While theories abound as to what actually caused the demise of the great King, the truth will remain shrouded in mystery forever. That there were those who would want him dead there can be no doubt. Could someone have poisoned his drink or food? The King was a robust young man who by rights should not have been felled by a fever, but on the other hand he had fallen into unhealthy habits

those who had been closest to the king in life hashed out the question of whether the Empire should remain intact according to Alexander's vision or be carved into pieces. The resulting "Wars of the Diadochi" or "successor wars" raged for twenty five years, until in 300 B.C. Alexander's Macedonian generals fought four major wars until at last the question was settled, and the Empire was divided.

in the year before his death. Malaria was not uncommon, and it could certainly be deadly. It should not be forgotten that Alexander had sustained several serious wounds in battle over the course of his campaigns and that these may have weakened his constitution or caused infection.

It seems likely that Alexander had not lost hope of recovery at any time. He did not call his advisors to deliberate on what should take place after his death. He did not name a successor. He simply slipped away, leaving chaos and confusion to reign, and his empire to essentially fall apart. His top generals carved up the territory among themselves, but it ceased to be a cohesive entity at the moment of Alexander's death.

Alexander had been larger than life. The length and breadth of his kingdom almost defy imagination even until today. His childhood dreams and visions had come to fruition and multiplied themselves! No reckless destroyer, he meant to build a new society in the realms he conquered. A new world order was the final plan, and perhaps it would have been realized had Alexander been

The conquered Macedonian territory became four distinct regions: Syria, Egypt, Asia Minor, and Macedonia. Four of Alexander's generals took over the rule of the divided empire. Ptolemy took over the rich territory of Egypt and Judea, perhaps the least sought after among the generals. Antipater kept the rule of Macedonia but passed it later to his son Cassander. Antigonus took over the reign of Syria, and Seleucius ruled in Babylonia.

granted a few more years. While he had defects and faults of character as any man, Alexander was principled and in his own way impeccably fair. He was a man of values, not just of power and might. As a result of Alexander's great adventure, the entire world was exposed to Greek ideas, Greek philosophy, and culture. The effects of that still resonate today all over the world, on continents Alexander did not know existed.

The story of Alexander stirs the hearts of men and women everywhere, and time will surely not dim the great King's glory, or tarnish his memory.

The year 321 B.C. marks the beginning of the Hellenistic period. Alexander was gone but the territories he conquered would never be the same. The dissemination of Greek culture, the Greek language, and the many progressive Greek institutions was of enormous influence which in fact continues to this day. Greece was no longer an isolated community and the East and West were forever mingled. Religion, art, science and philosophy all over the known world was influence by Greek thought as Greek culture became dominant in all corners of the Empire. This is Alexander's most abiding legacy.